CW00601541

Fear and Friendship

Fear and Friendship

Anglicans Engaging with Islam

Edited by
Frances Ward and Sarah Coakley

continuum

Continuum International Publishing Group
The Tower Building   80 Maiden Lane
11 York Road   Suite 704
London   New York
SE1 7NX   NY 10038

www.continuumbooks.com

© Frances Ward and Sarah Coakley, with the contributors, 2012

All rights reserved. No part of this publication may be reproduced or transmitted in any form or by any means, electronic or mechanical, including photocopying, recording or any information storage or retrieval system, without prior permission from the publishers.

First published 2012

British Library Cataloguing-in-Publication Data
A catalogue record for this book is available from the British Library.

ISBN: 978-1-4411-0149-5 (paperback)

Typeset by Fakenham Prepress Solutions, Fakenham, Norfolk NR21 8NN
Printed and bound in India

Contents

Foreword – Sarah Coakley   vii

Preface   xiii

1 *Fear and Friendship: Conversation or Conversion?* –
  Alex Hughes   3

2 *'Strangers and Neighbours': The Springfield Project and
  Barelwi Mosque Next Door* – Edmund Newey in
  conversation with Richard Sudworth   17

3 *From Identity Politics to Engagement: Making Sense of
  Muslim Communities in Britain* – Philip Lewis   39

4 *Islamophobia* – Nuzhat Ali   57

5 *Much Ado About Nothing at Bradford Cathedral* –
  Frances Ward   65

6 *Via Media* – Miriam Mushayi, Imran Manzoor and
  Javaad Alipoor   79

7 *The Importance of Offence: Satire, the Church of England
  and Islam* – Rachel Mann   91

8 *Giving Place: Exploring Christian Hospitality* – Ian Wallis   105

9 *Scriptural Reasoning* – Catriona Laing   118

10 *Hospitality in Prayer* – Judith, SLG   132

   Afterword – Rowan Williams, The Archbishop
   of Canterbury   145

   *A Note on the 2009 Littlemore Conference at
   St Andrew's, Handsworth* – Edmund Newey   153

Foreword

Sarah Coakley

This is a book about Islam in contemporary Britain, and its relation to the Anglican parish system. Since the genre of the book is novel, it is important to understand what it being attempted here, both theologically and politically, and what is at stake.

The Littlemore Group, which is responsible for this book, is made up of a number of Anglican clerics who have devoted themselves simultaneously to scholarship and to the demands of ordinary parish life. Our first book, *Praying for England*,[1] laid out a vision of what such a vocation might entail, and invited the reader to re-imagine the *representative* role of the parish priest in today's 'secularized' culture. Our theological writing is grounded first and foremost in the complexities and richness of what is happening to us day by day: in the parishes, schools, hospitals, cathedral precincts and other places we serve as ministers and theologians. Often we feel bemusement and surprise at the paradoxes of 'secularism' and its apparent opposites that we encounter here; often we find that the established categories of theological analysis are being stretched to their limits. Not least is this the case when the currently politically-charged issue of the relation between Christianity and Islam in this country is at stake, especially since the events of 9/11 and the London bombings of July 2005. This book faces head-on the political realities of a Britain in the throes of a new and alarming 'Islamophobia'.

Yet the central argument of this book is that the role of the Anglican parish cleric in brokering relations of hospitality, negotiation, friendship and debate between Christianity and Islam retains a deeper significance than is commonly realized. Despite (and perhaps partly because of) established Anglicanism's currently 'depotentiated' condition in a culture of vying religious convictions and none, its representative role and responsibility as the established Church remains.[2] Within the parish system itself (in which Muslim adherents may in some places now vastly outnumber practising Anglicans), and within the symbolically-laden realm of the city cathedrals, the story of British Muslim–Anglican relations is being worked out piece by piece. This book bears witness to that creative work in progress.

But first our volume has to explore the deep paradoxes of such work-on-the-ground. It is not uncommon today for Anglican clerics to find themselves transplanted to parishes with strong Muslim presences of *different* sorts, and to have little idea how to begin to broker relations with and between them. Battling with very survival can be a first, and even overwhelming, preoccupation for beleaguered Anglican congregations in such circumstances, as Alex Hughes poignantly outlines in the first essay in this book. The result can be an inward-looking perspective motivated by unspoken fear and defensiveness.

Simply finding the time to understand that there is 'no such thing as Islam-in-general' involves a steep learning curve which Philip Lewis's chapter in this book crucially sets out to help the reader negotiate. The sort of background information that Lewis here provides on the sheer diversity of British 'Islam', and on its internal theological, ethnic and political complexity, is a million miles away from older, and more sanitized, accounts of 'inter-faith relations', which moved counters around on the theological board as if they were discrete homogeneous units on an even spatial terrain. In retrospect, such an approach was as politically naïve as it was theologically presumptuous. Learning the *specificity* of local forms of British Islam – its theological assumptions, the training backgrounds of its *imams*, its social and financial aspirations and the prospects or lack thereof for its youth – is the prime task for any Anglican engagement of seriousness and depth. This book invites the reader into a number of such local adventures, both rich and strange.

But there is another, and perhaps yet more fundamental, challenge in consciousness needed for Anglicans to begin to respond graciously to the current religious ecology, even beyond the overcoming of a fundamental ignorance about British Islam which remains disturbingly prevalent. And this too has to be met head-on. It is the realization that, even as the number of practising Anglicans has 'bottomed out' statistically at the end of the 20th century, the institution of the Established Church still represents state *power* to those who are immigrant 'minorities'. The Anglican Church thus retains the more or less subliminal responsibility to play the 'host' – whether with care, prayerfulness and insight, or with fear, hostility and defensiveness. Numerous touching *vignettes* in this volume bear witness to this remainingly powerful sensibility on both sides, whether in Sr Judith's encounters with her gentle Sufi neighbours in the chip shop in east Oxford, or in Edmund Newey's account of the symbolic valency of the back steps of his church for drop-outs from both Sikh and Muslim communities in Handsworth, Birmingham. It is in such improvised encounters that spiritual mustard-seeds are sown for something greater, something of immense significance for the future of British culture and of its political stability. But what then *is* that 'greater' possibility of spiritual accord and peace to which this book witnesses?

The answer is that there is no *one* strategy or programme, whether political or theological, that can supply a simple answer to myriad, complex, changing local scenarios of Muslim–Christian encounter in today's Britian. That is why a book such as this, which presents to the reader a series of accounts of such ingenious local initiatives both Christian and Muslim, such unexpected growths in friendship and trust, and such highly practical projects of social assistance, may well fire the imagination more effectively than the enunciation of a series of generic theological or political principles. Often in these narratives, we find the most unexpected and counterintuitive twists and turns: the evangelical Mission church in Birmingham which ended up building a large day centre for its Muslim neighbours in Springfield with absolutely no interest in converting them; the Saudi student who set out to harangue or convert his local parish priest but in fact inspired him to say his own daily office *outside* his church building, as a quiet public witness of fidelity to the broken-down neighbourhood they both shared; the cathedral canon who hit on the extraordinary spiritual creativity of discussing inter-religious tensions with a group of Muslim women via the medium of a Shakespeare play; the Anglican priest-theologian who decided that the best use of a redundant urban church was to turn it into a mosque; the young Muslim who realized that members of his own community were becoming 'radicalized' more by a-political isolation and ignorance than by real political understanding and concern – and set out to do something about it with the aid of his friends and government money. Here are stories which suggest new and unexpected ways forward, new resources of hope and engagement.

So, as in *Praying for England*, this book sets much store by the means of its irreducible use of narrative. We have deliberately set Anglican voices here alongside a variety of Muslim ones, also; for it is only by listening as deeply as we can to the *unfamiliar* that new means of dialogue can emerge. In the face of a seemingly impossible or threatening political situation, the theological imagination needs rekindling, and the hope thereby restored. But such theological hope has to come equally from *both* sides of the religious 'divide', despite the political power differential that can never be occluded or denied: it is in having our Anglican identity held up to us afresh through the lens of the vision of the Muslim 'other' (in all its variety) that we may attain a new vision of our own heritage and its possibilities. If this book contributes in only a small way to such an emerging vision, it will more than adequately have fulfilled its task.

But, finally, there are at least two other, remaining, lessons that run through, and unite, the narratives in these pages. Again, they are counter-intuitive and paradoxical ones. The first insight is that the best way to engage in practices of friendship in a context of prevalent fear is not to *withdraw* from one's profoundest convictions, doctrines and spiritual practices, but to deepen them – in intentional gentleness and openness. We see this phenomenon borne witnessed to in Catriona Laing's challenging account of shared 'Scriptural Reasoning' (inter-faith meditation on authoritative texts) in the parish and beyond, just as much as in Sr Judith's remarkable story of how a local Muslim community came to share silence with the members of a contemplative Anglican convent in Oxford. It is important to stress, as these authors do with the deepest realism, that such daring encounters can and do go *wrong* on occasions; but as with any adventure into the realm of the new and the unknown, that is the price to pay in following the allure of the Spirit, 'who blows where it wills'.

The second abiding theme is connected to this, and involves a certain offence to the 'political correctness' which can often afflict 'liberal' Anglicanism, even despite its own best intentions. It is that the opposite of fear and hostility is not the suppression of uncomfortable and contentious issues for the sake of a false kind of relativistic stand-off. If theological *truth* is at stake, as it manifestly is in these pages, then a certain spiritual fearlessness must have the courage of its own convictions. Any anodyne withdrawal from debate on the grounds of a pale 'toleration' (in fact, often a cloak for covert forms of political hegemony, as history has shown) is a *faux* option which the authors of this book resist uncompromisingly. This is an undeniably difficult road to negotiate, as Rachel Mann's contribution to this volume illustrates above all; but it is doubtful that it can be ridden at all without the aid of the more demanding spiritual practices that our various traditions have handed down to us. Such are not practices of rigid boundary-making, hatred and division, but of vulnerability, surprise and change. 'Deep calls to deep', as the Psalmist says.

*

In the period since the July 2005 bombings, successive British governments – both Labour and Coalition – have responded with attempts to 'prevent' and 'contain' the political radicalization of Islamic youth in Britain. Such was the eminently understandable political reaction to a frightening reality; but its attempts to transmute into a truly 'theological' understanding of the situation on the ground have come only more recently, and somewhat haltingly. Meanwhile, official Anglican work on Anglican-Muslim relations has progressed in some promising ways;[3] but arguably there is a need for yet further *theological* bolstering and acuity: it seems the fear still lurks that a robustly theological discussion might be branded 'dogmatic', or 'hegemonic'. As Rowan Williams pertinently remarks in the Afterword to this volume: 'sustaining a universal claim about healing and meaning *without resorting to the tools of control or manipulation* is a ... calling that takes a lifetime to learn'.

This book then is a first attempt at giving such a lifetime's undertaking a set of concrete manifestations and a theological rationale. If it can inspire a future generation of clerics, ordinands and lay-people to similar, local endeavours of mutual engagement and transformation it will have served its modest purpose. As the Prophet says: 'The believer is the mirror of his fellow believer' (Bayhaqi, no. 17016). This book proposes that it is our job to make that a reality.

Notes

1 Samuel Wells and Sarah Coakley, eds, *Praying for England: Priestly Presence in Contemporary Culture* (London: Continuum, 2008).

2 This was a central theme of *Praying for England*: see especially Grace Davie's contribution, 'Debate', ibid, 147–70.

3 One thinks especially of *Presence and Engagement: The Churches' Task in a Multi Faith Society* (London: Church House Publishing, 2005), and *Generous Love: The Truth of the Gospel and the Call to Dialogue* (The Anglican Consultative Council, 2008).

Preface

In January 2011 Baroness Sayeeda Warsi gave the Sir Sigmund Sternberg lecture at University of Leicester. She was widely reported to claim that Islamophobia is now normal amongst the chattering middle classes and at their dinner parties. Islamophobia – fear of Islam – endemic within British society. Of course, the fact that the media failed to report the many constructive and valuable points she also made is part of the problem. Whether at the dinner table, or in society at large, we live with increasing polarizations, often fuelled by the media; none more so, perhaps, than between the 'West' and 'Islam'. The West and the Rest it has been called; the clash of civilisations is increasingly set to become a self-fulfilling prophecy.

Fear operates in many ways. There is the fear of the unknown, born of uncertainty and insecurity. There is the fear that the polarization is deepening, accompanied by a sense of confusion about what to do to create resilience in society to counter it. There is a very basic fear of causing offence: saying or doing the wrong thing. Fear feeds on division, and builds reinforcements in tribal ways: mentalities that rely upon the difference between us and them. You see it also when Muslims refer to everyone else as 'non-Muslims': basic distinctions are made on the basis of faith and religious allegiance in order to foster a sense of security.

This book offers diverse approaches in the engagement between the Church of England and Islam, and a sense of feeling the way. We read of creative strategies, some more developed than others, but all with *a sense of uncertainty, of proceeding without a compass, unsure of what the map is. The editors hope that the reader will appreciate these different perspectives and approaches, to emerge with a greater under- standing of the largely uncharted ground before us as a nation learning to live together with peace and justice, in friendship and trust. And so the differences in approach, style and content between the authors are not homogenized: we have offered explanations where necessary as each contributor has attempted to move from fear to friendship.*

The first two chapters belong together, each written from the perspective of Anglican parish priests. In the first, Alex Hughes describes his personal response to the approach of Mohammed, a young Muslim living in his parish who seeks to engage with Christianity. Alex wonders aloud about the encounter as they meet on several occasions, as he also wonders about the future of his parish church in inner city Portsmouth. The second chapter presents a very different scene, in Springfield, Birmingham, and highlights how a parish has addressed the social issues for young people of the area, working closely with the Barelwi Mosque next door.

There is no blueprint for such encounters. Alex responds as a priest, open but unsure where this may lead. The Springfield Project, too, has developed with an open mind, recognizing the need for engagement and trusting the friendships that grow.

1

Fear and Friendship: Conversation or Conversion?

Alex Hughes

Alex Hughes writes here of his encounter with Mohammed, one which begins in theological stalemate and grows into friendship. It is written against a background in which the confidence and certainty of Mohammed's stance on Islam seems reflected in its local prominence, while the threadbare nature of the local Anglican presence finds its echo in Alex's cautious and slightly indirect equivocations and qualifiers on faith. But, as the relationship with Mohammed develops, the richness of Alex's deliberate poverty, his empty hands, becomes plain, transforming into a sense of gift and possibility: for (as he reminds us) friendship, like worship, is not for use but for joy.

The parishes of St Peter's and St Luke's, Southsea, where I have been priest-in-charge since October 2008, are in the heart of Portsmouth. Although they take in the university, law courts, guildhall and civic offices, as well as pockets of high-value housing, they cover one of the most densely populated and poorest parts of Hampshire, scoring highly on most indices of deprivation. The churches themselves have been declining for decades: I once presided at a 'Family Communion' to which only three people came, two of them late (tardy, not dead). One parish has a seriously dilapidated building, no lay officers and only one parishioner regularly attending worship;[1] the other is cash-strapped but sustained by a small group of devoted lay folk who work incredibly hard to 'keep the show on the road', though barely any of them are parishioners. From the outside both churches look as if they might have gone out of business, and the local community pays them scant regard.

On the eastern edge of the parishes, in a very prominent position – far more prominent than either of my churches or any other religious site in the area – is the newly face-lifted and refurbished Jami mosque. The mosque is a recent acquisition, following a split within the city's Sunni community. In addition to two prayer halls, one each for men and women, the mosque comprises a suite of offices and school rooms. It comes across as a bustling religious community, given its prominent location and the conspicuous flux of prayer-capped men and women in various forms of distinctively Islamic clothing. Even though the Jami mosque has a reputation for being closed to outsiders, and only 8 per cent of the parishes' population are Muslim, I would guess that many local people could more easily identify the whereabouts of the mosque than either parish church.

Perhaps because of my preoccupation with the fate of my churches, and the demand of this exercise to focus on the Muslim presence in my area, I may have under- and overstated respectively the fortunes of church and mosque. For the purposes of my reflection, however, this may not be a bad thing: perception is often more significant than reality, especially when comparative self-perception is involved. The plain truth is that, as I have pondered how the Church of England might better engage with Islam, I have come to recognize how little this is a matter of concern to me at the level of my day-to-day ministry. Although one of the things that attracted me back into the Anglican fold in my late teens was its vaunted spirit of hospitality, I question now how that is, or might be, put into practice in my situation.

If the demands of parish ministry mean that I am not greatly intent on pursuing relations with my Muslim neighbours, one such has been eager to pursue me. He introduced himself – minus his give-away name – via an answerphone request for answers to some questions he had about Christianity. Unabashed evangelist that I am, I called him at once and we arranged to meet for coffee.

Mohammed opened, in typical Arab style, with sincere enquiries about my family's well-being. He then moved on swiftly to ask what I thought about Sikh cow-worship. I replied that I did not think that, strictly speaking, Sikhs do *worship* cows; but I was glad when he decided not to continue with this topic, as I felt a little out of my depth. Perhaps he was, too. In any case, it quickly transpired that the point of his gambit was to assess my capacity to distinguish between truth and falsehood in religious matters, as a preamble to testing the relative merits of Christianity and Islam. I have yet to satisfy him on this score.

One of the reasons why I like Mohammed is that, as a passionate advocate of his religion – he is a postgraduate student from Saudi Arabia – he reminds me of myself, as I was in my early teens. Back then I was utterly convinced of the cogency and objectivity of my arguments for the truth of Christianity, which were largely predicated on the truth of the Bible. For certain, I thought, any intellectually honest enquirer after religious truth should come round to my position. Alas, many did not; and in time, neither did I. There then followed a period in my late teens when I debated vigorously with some of my co-religionists precisely in order to refute my former stance. After a few years I gave this up as a bad job: the argument never seemed to go anywhere. And I find the same with Mohammed. He is adamant that if I treat his claims for the finality of the Qur'an without prejudice I will submit to its authority. I, however, am deeply prejudiced, by which I mean that I don't accept the terms of his approach. Despite his assertions to the contrary, I believe that there is a 'hidden move' in Mohammed's apology for (Sunni) Islam, which is his prior commitment to its truth. As our conversations have continued I have tried to talk this through with him, as I will explain later.

I have to confess that I found our first couple of meetings rather stultifying, as Mohammed continued to try to engage me on his own terms. I began to wonder whether I might politely 'drop' him, until things shifted slightly at our third meeting. He began as usual by asking me a question designed to elicit an answer which he could criticize within his preferred framework. Fortunately a waitress arrived at that moment, and we were distracted. I took advantage of the hiatus to ask a question of my own. How did Mohammed become a Muslim? It was my first real opportunity to introduce a story-telling element into our conversations. I can't say it was very successful, for we soon reverted to our old dialectical exchange. But by the time we paid our bill I felt that something had changed: our discussion was perhaps a bit less abstract; we had touched tentatively on the part played by will, desire and aesthetic sensibility in religious faith; we even talked around the formative significance of history, culture and upbringing. Maybe what happened was that for the first time we talked together about what it is like to be a religious *person*, rather than about religion in some abstract sense. I think this was the start of our journey towards a friendship of sorts.

At our most recent meeting, for example, after our usual pleas-antries, Mohammed started telling me about the trouble he was having with his academic studies, and we went on to talk about how the sense of purpose he derives from his faith helps him to persevere. This led further as we shared our common experience as people of faith of the challenge posed by widespread indifference to 'meaning' and 'purpose'. For a moment we found that faith drew us together, even though the substance of our faith is very different. Perhaps it is because of moments like this that, although the awkward question of conversion, or 'reversion', remains steadfastly 'on the table' between us as we sip our coffee, that question is not something we feel obliged either to ignore or to fear, since we can in some ways identify with one another, despite the gulf that separates us. If anything, the challenge posed by the possibility of conversion/reversion means that our friendship is not evasive, but frank and honest, especially when it comes to matters of faith.

In fact, as I think about it now, it is probably fair to say that I speak more freely about my personal faith with Mohammed than with any of 'the faithful' who belong to my churches (among whom the conversation turns more often than not to matters of institutional survival). This is an unexpected gift. I would also add that Mohammed's frankness about his intentions towards me has meant that our discussions have not been hampered by a felt need to tiptoe around each other's religious sensibilities. This has been quite liberating for me, since I am far from being anything like an 'interfaith guru', and generally fear to tread on such politically-sensitive ground. Furthermore, I actually think that my only other sustained engagement with a Muslim neighbour – a fairly liberal Shia – suffered from a lack of forthrightness about our differences: it put friendship *before* faithfulness in a way that actually militated against building the kind of quality relationship I enjoy with Mohammed. I wonder whether it is sometimes tempting, or politically expedient, to acquiesce in a superficial friendship which prevents the development of a hard-won companionship.

Another way in which my time with Mohammed has become more fruitful is through the attention we give to our scriptures. Though I had no direct experience of 'scriptural reasoning', I wondered whether our dialogue might be helped if we actually spent time together looking at our sacred texts. Mohammed was delighted when I suggested this, and since then our meetings have always included study of the Bible and the Qur'an. (Mohammed's Arabic Bible now has more marginal notes and highlighted passages than the battered RSV study edition I have been using for the last 18 years.)

Because Mohammed is keen to show me the error of my Christian ways, he has unashamedly chosen Qur'anic texts that criticize elements of Christian belief (he went straight for the theological jugular by giving me Surah 19 'Maryam/Mary' and Surah 5 'Al-Maeda/The Feast', which accuse Christianity of polytheism with respect to the doctrine of the Trinity and devotion to Mary). I in turn have selected passages from the Bible which I think help to show why Christians believe what they do (I countered with John's prologue and chapter 14). There is insufficient space here to elaborate on all of the scriptures we have discussed, but two have proved particularly fruitful.

I wrote earlier about the kind of religious apologetic that rests almost exclusively on demonstrating the 'truth' of scripture. In the course of our conversations it has become apparent that I am not the

first Christian with whom Mohammed has engaged in this way, and
that some of his previous interlocutors have been happy to play tit for
tat with him, by pitting the veracity of the Bible against the Qur'an.
My challenge, therefore, has been to try to tease out why I think the
church's relationship to the Bible is different from Islam's relationship
to the Qur'an.

Mohammed has been rather taken aback by my willingness to
concede that the Bible is full of errors and contradictions, and has
found it hard to understand why this does not lead me to abandon
my faith. It has also been a challenge to me to articulate a coherent
account of my position. To be honest, I have not satisfied either of
us on this front, though it has spurred me on to read and reflect
more deeply on the subject – which is really to say that, in trying to
explain myself to Mohammed, I have discovered my own theological
ignorance and ineptitude. There is a real danger here that I might
try to withdraw from or evade certain avenues in our conversation
from fear of exposure; and I do realize that my position must seem
weak to Mohammed. I'm not really sure how to handle this, except
to speak as truthfully and with as much integrity as I can (which is
harder than one might imagine given what is at stake in our robust
conversations).

Although I'm sure Mohammed thinks my view of scripture leaves
me vulnerable to conversion/reversion, I can tell that he is also
intrigued by a faith that does not work in the same way as his own.
Probably the best conversation we have had on this topic arose from
our reading of John 14–16, especially the texts relating to the 'Spirit
of truth', which led us on to what I described as 'the birthday of the
church' at Pentecost (Acts 2). Through this shared reading I was able
to talk about the strange dynamic in which the Spirit-inspired church
is historically prior to the inspiration of the Christian scriptures, yet
accepts their priority. Trying to explain this to Mohammed felt a bit
like juggling blancmange, and made me very conscious of the way
in which I am 'on show', and in some sense performing on behalf of
the whole church when I talk to him. It was not at all comfortable to
become so acutely aware of my stammering witness, and I can well

imagine that I might have ducked the challenge had I been less sure of our friendship. I console myself with the rather commonplace thought that it is only through allowing oneself to be vulnerable that new dimensions of relationship are opened up. Perhaps there are aspects of Islam that Mohammed finds difficult to make sense of, too. Maybe one day he will talk to me about them. Not altogether unrelated to this is that, at my suggestion, we have made a shared mental note to talk about the question of violence in the name of religion. Given the sensitivity of the subject I would never dare to broach it normally, but I feel confident that my relationship with Mohammed is secure enough for us to be able to discuss it in a fairly forthright manner.

I have already indicated that underlying the discussions Mohammed and I have about our respective scriptures is a fundamental question about the pursuit of truth – or Truth, as I am sure he would write it. The most promising conversation we have had about this emerged from our reading of Surah 5, which tells the story of how Allah certified the prophetic message of Jesus by sending down a feast from heaven to dispel any lingering doubts among his followers. I asked Mohammed whether Allah still provides such miraculous reassurances for hesitating faith. He thought not, because they are only necessary to establish the credentials of Allah's chosen prophets, of whom Mohammad was the last. I then recounted the story of 'doubting Thomas', ending with Jesus' words, 'Have you believed because you have seen me? Blessed are those who have not seen and yet believe' (John 20.29). We did not hesitate to agree that in this respect we are both more blessed than the first disciples. But then I wondered what it was that led us to our faith? How do we know our faith is true? And, more pertinently, how might we be persuaded of its falsehood?

As I anticipated, Mohammed launched into an account of the logical and evidential process by which the truth-claims of the Qur'an may be established beyond reasonable doubt. When it was my turn to speak, I told Mohammed that I often feel in our discussions on this subject that 'I am playing football while you are playing rugby'. When he asked me to explain what I meant by this I realized I was about to get out of my intellectual depth (and that a considerable strain was going to be put on the discussion by Mohammed's limited English). To the best of my ability I tried to relate the history of Western philosophy, leading to modern and post-modern scepticism. I was very impressed by Mohammed's ability to follow what I was saying, and surprised by the humility with which he acknowledged the possible weakness of his approach. He said he would go away and do some reading on this before we next met, though as I write, our conversation has been deferred because of his need to concentrate on his studies. But it clearly raises some big questions for anyone engaged in conversation with, or attempting the conversion of, someone whose faith is different from one's own. What is truth? How do we recognize it? How should we pursue it? Or is 'truth' an unhelpful or erroneous category from which we need to be delivered? And the simple truth is that, although I have some idea about how one might think about these questions, I don't know the answers. Without fully understanding the sophisticated work that has been written on these matters, I sense that my faith is in some sense 'groundless' – or at least grounded in the grace of a God who cannot conveniently be placed on the table between Mohammed and me for inspection. So how can we talk about the rightness or truth of our respective faiths? Where do we begin? As yet we have not really grappled with this problem at an intellectual level, except insofar as I think we are both able to see that it *is* a problem. What I will say, though, is that despite the difficulty of knowing how to pursue truth, our growing friendship means that Mohammed and I try not to flinch from speaking truthfully. Perhaps this is a start.

A few months ago Mohammed returned to Saudi Arabia, having finished his course of study. Although he told me of his plans to return for further study I have not seen him since. If he comes back, I will be pleased to resume our meetings, but the current (temporary, I hope) end of our active engagement gives me the chance to reflect more generally on how it has affected me.

As I explained at the beginning, I am very conscious of the relative public profiles of church and mosque in my parishes, and

Mohammed's confident approach to me, with its explicit agenda and robust challenge, has only served to reinforce my perception. This has had some small practical consequences, as well as providing material for further reflection.

Probably the most obvious response to the feeling that my churches are largely invisible and ignored, and overshadowed by the life of the mosque, has been that, for the last 18 months, my colleague and I have prayed the daily offices outside the church building. It would be our normal practice to pray bodily – standing and sitting, making the sign of the cross, bowing for the 'Glory be', and perhaps even nodding at the name of 'Jesus' – and we have made this a feature of our praying outside, too. Our aim has been to bear witness to a living spiritual tradition, with a discipline of regular and ordered prayer (drawing an obvious parallel with Islam). For similar reasons I have encouraged the congregation to decorate the *outside* of the church building as a sign of the life within. Apart from opening up a new line in Sunday school craft-work, anecdotal evidence suggests that this has provoked interest and enjoyment in the local community, and perhaps gone some way towards putting the churches back on people's mental map of the area. I also sense that it has engendered a new confidence among some of the laity, as well as releasing creativity: I never know what to expect when I approach the church building, especially when seasonal changes are due. More recently my two churches have joined forces to consider our long-term options with respect to our physical presence in the parishes. I am reluctant to go into much detail on this front because our plans are embryonic, but suffice it to say that we want to create a more adequate home for the church, in which to gather and to offer hospitality, and we want to be a more conspicuous centre of spirituality. It would be disingenuous of me to claim that all of these developments have arisen only as a result of my encounter with Mohammed and the high profile of the mosque, but the proximity of a flourishing Muslim community, and the confidence of my Muslim friend, have certainly been a spur to self-review and action.

At a personal and ministerial level I think that my time spent with Mohammed has helped to reawaken an element in my sense of vocation of which I had largely lost sight. Although I continue to find elements of my younger, more evangelistic self unattractive and unconvincing, Mohammed's uncompromising apology for Islam jerked me out of an almost exclusively liturgical and pastoral conception of ministry: I found myself having to think about the case for Christianity (so to speak). Perhaps this would have happened anyway as I continued to contemplate my depleted congregations. But the point is that my conversation with Mohammed, which constantly circled the question of conversion, has made me more alert to the problem of how we commend faith. I have been led to think about the paradigm shift that has taken place in recent years in the church's understanding of mission, from an approach that makes worship the entry point into the life of faith, with fellowship coming after ('believing before belonging'), to a more relational style, which seeks to build friendship as a bridge to sharing faith ('belonging before believing'). For many this is now commonplace, but the reality is that struggling parishes like mine often become so intensely focused on survival that there is no appetite for engaging with others for the sake of Christian mission, let alone reaching out to another religious community. There is a danger that the steadily contracting purview of many churches, as they focus more and more on survival at the expense even of propagation, renders them increasingly incapable of expressing their vocation to hospitality. Perhaps, then, the question of hospitality towards Islam should be set within a wider debate about the vocation, mission and organization of the Church of England as Christendom wanes, establishment unravels and society becomes increasingly pluralist and multicultural.

Much has been written about the church's rediscovery of life at the margins of society, which Islam and other religious traditions in this country have long inhabited. It is intriguing to imagine what a marginalized Established Church might offer to the nation, if such a doubtful position could be 'secured'. This is part of my daily reality as the leader of an ignored or disparaged church within a largely leaderless, ignored and disparaged community, surrounded by powerful, monopolizing organizations such as the council and the university. But it is not altogether clear to me how this reality may be converted into a renewed sense of generous-hearted companionship, rather than a more or less reactionary defensiveness. I do not mean to suggest that a self-conscious embracing of 'the margins' is mere theological romanticism – after all, it is where Jesus spent his ministry – but it probably requires a spirituality deeper than mine to find enrichment in obscurity. I might also add that, rightly or wrongly, there is a widespread feeling that while Christianity is being squeezed from the public arena, other faith traditions are being amply accommodated. This is not in fact my experience, and I cannot imagine that any of my local Muslim contacts would express satisfaction with their current position. What I have found, however, is that while some Christians look with renewed hope to a church shorn of its historic privileges, many Muslims aspire to an ascendant Islam. Never in my experience has this been expressed in the ideological terms of Islamism; but there is certainly no idealization of socio-political obscurity.

What does all of this amount to? Until recently the Church of England perhaps felt it could afford to be generous towards people of faith other than Christians, since it did not doubt its predominance. But many parts of the church now face a different reality, as may be seen in the story of my engagement with Islam. Although Muslims make up a minority of the local population in my parishes, they are the most visibly active religious community, and it is partly from them that I have learned to make the spiritual life of my churches more conspicuous. Again, although I am (probably) the best-known local faith-leader, it was a visiting foreign student who took the initiative in seeking me out and trying to secure my reversion to Islam, and who has provoked me to think again about the importance of sharing faith in and through hospitality. And yet there have also been times when Mohammed sought from me a pastoral ministry of listening and sharing, as, for example, when he struggled with his work and the challenge of living faithfully in a society that is generally indifferent to religion. What I see, therefore, is an assortment of paradoxes surrounding the interaction of Christianity

and Islam. As a Church of England minister I have a certain prominence in the community, and yet I am cramped by sensitivity to
political correctness and the inward-looking focus of church life,
as well as by elements of my theological and intellectual formation
which make me cautious about asserting my own position. By
contrast, my Muslim neighbours seem to display a measure of
commitment, confidence and conviction that belies their minority
status. This raises questions about the distribution of power and
strength, whether real or perceived, which can be disconcerting. As
I have tried to show in this account of my own experience, although
I certainly don't see Islam as a *threat*, particularly in the light of my
developing friendship with Mohammed, my engagement has carried
me outside my 'comfort zone' and left me feeling exposed and inade-
quate at times. This leads me to one final issue that continues to press
upon my mind.

I have tried to stress the importance of speaking truthfully, and
yet I am aware that there may be a fundamental falsehood underlying my conversations with Mohammed, depending on whether
either of us ever seriously entertains the possibility that we might
convert/revert. If we don't, then what have we been doing? In
pondering this I am reminded of something Rowan Williams has
said about theological integrity: 'Discourse that conceals is discourse
that (consciously or not) sets to foreclose the possibility of a genuine
response ... A two-level discourse is one which steps back from the
risks of *conversation* – above all from those two essential features of
conversation, the recognition of an "unfinished" quality in what has
been said on either side, and the possibility of correction.'[2] Thus, I
think, it becomes impossible to maintain a clear distinction between
conversation and conversion, which poses a challenge to my faithfulness, both as a person of faith and as a friend. Fear of loss, the
price of friendship and the risk of conversation all tumble into one
another when brought within the horizon of conversion.

Maybe one way to maintain some kind of orientation from within
the Christian tradition is to consider that the baptismal *metanoia*
operates within a greater framework of *eucharistia*. The radical turn

to God only becomes possible when it is grounded in gratitude – or perhaps better, when it knows its 'groundlessness', because, like everything else, it is *given*. Only an attitude of thankful dependence can overcome the fear of loss which makes one recoil from such risky ventures as true conversation, and from sincere friendship too.

I am back now to where I started, wondering how to handle the experience of scarcity that so easily reduces faithful living to an inward-looking, pragmatic utilitarianism, unwilling to bear the cost of stepping outside the familiar, or welcoming the stranger. Against this background, meeting with Mohammed is not a very productive exercise: there is no obvious 'return' from my 'investment' of time and energy in building our relationship. But isn't that the point (though 'point' doesn't quite seem like the right word)? For surely at the very moment my friendship becomes ensnared in a web of utility, my friend becomes an instrument of my own selfish will or desire?

By contrast, true friendship can and should be a sacrament or icon of the gratuitous, creative being of God, which has no point, and serves no purpose, but simply overflows from the joy of God's life as a Trinity of love. As such, friendship is akin to worship (an entirely and properly useless activity), and companionship is rightly seen as eucharistic. 'It is in eating and talking together that we celebrate our joy and gratitude for life and creation, and share our concern about all that mars these gifts of God.'[3]

Notes

1 Since Advent 2009 we no longer worship in the parish church. We now have a 'house church' on a weekday evening, and run a drop-in outreach programme in the community room of a tower block on Sunday mornings.
2 Rowan Williams, *On Christian Theology* (Oxford: Blackwell, 2000), pp. 3–4.
3 Adapted from Sr Maureen Henderson, *Friends on the Way* (Peterborough: Epworth Press, 1999), p. 46. Quoted by E. D. H. Carmichael, *Friendship: Interpreting Christian Love* (London: T&T Clark, 2004), p. 196.

2

'Strangers and Neighbours': The Springfield Project and Barelwi Mosque Next Door

Edmund Newey in conversation with Richard Sudworth

Two Anglican priests from different traditions within Anglicanism reflect together on how they might understand the foundations and the outworkings of their grounded vocation in the areas in which they minister. One, Handsworth, is an area of ethnic and religious diversity; the other, Springfield, is predominantly Muslim. Their discussion centres on the Springfield Project, a Christian and church-based social initiative for families, unique in Birmingham and both welcomed and effective in its area. As Edmund and Richard consider what they do, each finds in the inclusiveness of the Anglican 'cure of souls', and in the Hookerian vision of Christ in every neighbour, an abiding and lively model for a ministry of confident, attentive and vulnerable Christian presence.

[Edmund Newey writes:] *The church steps at St Andrew's, Handsworth, are a popular gathering place for small groups of people on the margins of local life. As often as not, on arriving at church you find a teenage couple, a pair of residents from a local hostel or a small group of Muslim or Sikh men drinking cheap lager from a can in a paper bag. Principally they go there for concealment, but, talking with them, there is also a surprising degree of respect for the building and those who*

*come to worship in it. And from time to time the worship inside spills
out onto the steps.*

*Last week I met 'Nick' again, a nominal Muslim man in his late
30s. About six months ago, he had been in quite a state on the steps:
worrying about having no money to buy his son's birthday present
or even to travel to see him. I had thought that a carefully fabricated
begging story was to follow, but I had been wrong. What he had wanted
was a prayer and a blessing, and I had obliged. Six months later he and I
both assumed that we would have forgotten that event, but we had not:
I had remembered for the unworthy reason that it was a rare occasion
when a tale about having no money had not ended in a request for a
tenner; but Nick had remembered on the much better grounds that the
day of the blessing had, in his own words, been 'one of the best days of
his life'. Everything had gone right for him: a friend had 'borrowed him
50 quid', he'd bought his present, seen his son, and even got on well with
his estranged partner. What's more, he had told all his friends what had
happened. Suddenly I realized why an old but still serviceable DVD
player had appeared on those same church steps a few months back:
it had been a thanks offering from Nick. In a small way the steps had
become a place of liturgical exchange – and the unworthiness of the
minister and his thoughts had not hindered the effect of the blessing!*

*I tell this story as a miniature version of the sort of transform-
ative encounter that has been unfolding on a much larger and
more systematic scale at the Springfield Project on the other side of
Birmingham. My meeting on the steps is the sort of mustard seed
from which sturdy trees like the Springfield Project may grow. At the
project's heart is a publicly funded children's centre, but, uniquely in
Birmingham, it is also a faith-based children's centre with a vision
to engage with other religious groups – and in particular the local
majority Muslim community. It has a very strong volunteer base and
has become trusted in the local area, and as a result people from many
different cultural and religious communities make use of its services.
It is also pioneering interfaith youth activities in partnership with a
variety of national bodies such as Scripture Union, Youth Encounter
and the Christian Muslim Forum, as well as with schools and mosques.*

This chapter traces an ongoing conversation between Richard Sudworth (the former chair of the Springfield Project) and me (the vicar of St Andrew's, Handsworth), in which we explore the motivations, methods and muddles of Christian mission in our respective areas. The contexts in which we work are both inner-urban and multicultural, but whereas Springfield is characterized by a numerically dominant Muslim community, Handsworth is ethnically and religiously much more mixed. It has a large and confident Sikh presence, but an equally significant African-Caribbean community and growing numbers of refugees and asylum seekers from Africa and the Middle East, as well as migrant workers from Eastern Europe. Richard and I come from markedly different Anglican traditions; our contexts have as much to set them apart as they have in common. Yet, rejoicing as we both do in the blessings and challenges of ministry and mission in our different multi-faith contexts, we continue to listen out for the particular vocation of our established Church of England in such places. What follows is a reflection on the ways in which two Anglican parishes, at different stages in the evolution of their mission, may heed that calling in confidence, humility and integrity, serving and being served by, challenging and being challenged by the communities in which they are set.

EN: The title of our chapter is 'Strangers and Neighbours'. One of the great insights of the Springfield Project and your reflections on it is your appreciation of the need to acknowledge strangeness both before and during the growth of neighbourliness between Muslims and Anglicans.

RS: The original impulse behind the Springfield Project was a period of renewed enthusiasm around the gathered worship of the church. The church had been growing and St Christopher's had become a hub for Christian worship in that area of the city. A persistent challenge was that the energy to worship had to translate into an engagement with the local Muslim-majority community if it was to mean anything. The significance of this is that Christian worship is somehow in the DNA of the stay-and-play, family support, nursery and other services of the Springfield Project.

The project did not begun with an assumption that common ground must be sought or that all faiths were essentially on the same path. As relationships have been forged, though, and deepening connections made with the community, shared goals have been discovered and commonalities affirmed.

Looking back at the Springfield Project story, it seems that there have been junctures in the church's life when that originating impulse to Christian worship could have been lost and the community engagement could have collapsed into an anonymous social enterprise. Equally, the confidence of the worshipping community could have become hectoring and strident without the learning and vulnerability that inevitably happens as relationships deepen across boundaries. Out of a Sunday morning congregation of around 130, approximately 40 adults either work for or volunteer in the Springfield Project at some point during a week. This means that the bringing together of Christian and Muslim stories is more than just an abstract concept. Lives are being shared, friendships made, differences discovered and profound concerns echoed.

The Catholic missiologist Stephen Bevans talks of the 'liturgy after the liturgy': the offering that we make as a Christian community from the generative life of the Eucharist into our day-to-day existence. For St Christopher's, I recognize how there has been a tangible interplay between the worship of the church and the dynamic of the community action. It has echoes of Michael Barnes' theology of interfaith relations with its cycle of worship and action that are mutually transforming.

EN: The liturgy changes everything, doesn't it? Gathered to meet Christ in the spiritual flesh and blood of the sacrament, we are sent out to greet him in the physical flesh and blood of his world. One of the habits of a church like St Andrew's is the daily celebration of the Eucharist. Sociologically, this might seem a poor thing: a handful of predominantly elderly folk pursuing a pattern of

personal devotion. But, theologically, a hasty judgement like that could scarcely be wider of the mark. Almost always it is the daily attendees at the Eucharist who relate best to the 'Nicks' of our area and who have the clearest picture of how the universal gospel should be put into local practice. Until dementia forced her retirement from frontline service, one 90-year-old member of our congregation set a shining example of just the kind of faithful and attentive ministry among 'all sorts and conditions of men [and women]' that is Anglicanism at its best. Equally ready to own her Christian faith in word and deed, Eleanor was a much-loved figure on the streets of the parish and, even veiled by illness, glimmers of that gifting still shine through in her nursing home. I am quite sure that the habits of a lifetime's worship have shaped her into the person she is.

The stirring words of Archbishop Frank Weston are always worth recalling: 'You cannot claim to worship Jesus in the Tabernacle, if you do not pity Jesus in the slum.' But that celebrated sentence depends on an equally uncompromising prior assertion of the duty and joy of worshipping Christ in the liturgy. Rowan Williams has commented about the need for a much more robust defence of the supernatural, God-initiated side of our church life, drawing attention to the significance of the sacraments as they create the Church week by week. As in Springfield, the best and most lasting mission and ministry projects in our parish have all arisen out of worship and they tend to be staffed by those who are faithful attendees at the Eucharist. The Friday Friends Stay and Play Group, the ecumenical Welcome Project for asylum seekers, even the apparently humble Thursday Coffee Morning: these are all 'liturgies after the liturgy', though perhaps less self-consciously so than they might be.

RS: St Christopher's has exemplified something of this dynamic in very practical ways. While the new children's centre was being built, replacing the church hall, the project's services all had to be provided from the church itself. Thus, Muslim parents were expected to leave their young children at a nursery within the sacred space of a church with all its traditional symbolism. The symbolic 'difference' of the cross could not be avoided. Rather than this becoming an obstacle to the Springfield Project, it became a natural tool for the telling of the story of the Christian community. Paradoxically, Muslim parents, in particular, felt more released to be themselves because the resonances of faith, prayer and sacred text were readily apparent. If the Christian community were relaxed about who *they* were in such a mixed setting, then Muslims could be relaxed about the public face of their own identity. Similarly, during the year that all the services of the project were housed in the church, Sunday morning worship could not avoid the freight of nursery toys, children's paintings and all the cultural images of the diversity of the project, Monday to Friday. Coming in to worship on a Sunday morning, the names of children such as Adil, Hafsa and Zakiya on display boards were bound to impress upon the church community the context of the 'liturgy after the liturgy'.

In specific relationships, too, church staff and volunteers were entering the homes of Muslim friends and vice versa. What it meant to declare Jesus as Lord in the creed on Sunday was being opened up by the confidence and resilience of Muslims who sought to bring their faith to bear in every aspect of *their* lives. The faithful do seem most open to working together.

Yet this process is naturally fragile and fraught with vulnerability. The respective histories of Christian–Muslim relations contain many skeletons in the cupboard. The colonial legacy and ongoing Islamophobia make many Muslims wary of the motives behind church-based interventions. Even so, defaulting to the simplistic power blocs of the Christian West and Islamic Orient would belie the actual complexity of relations. In many ways, St Christopher's parish is indicative of a truer ambiguity of power relations that requires *mutual* vulnerability. The Springfield Project is arguably a Christian 'host', yet we are very aware that the Christian presence in this part of the inner city is one of guests to a dominant Muslim community. The global motifs of Palestine, Afghanistan, 9/11, 2001 and 7/7, 2005 all offer potential rallying points that could create fissures between Christians and Muslims that would cut both ways. The Church of England remains established by the law of the state yet is increasingly marginalized in power and numbers in a sometimes aggressively secularizing public square. The motif of hospitality is naturally significant to any Christian understanding of the engagement with the 'stranger' but the Springfield Project testifies to the reciprocity of this hospitality where the church acts both as host *and* guest.

The Anglican document *Generous Love* rightly highlights the idea that the Eucharist, at the centre of the church, propels us to welcome and share in an economy of gift, while in turn receiving dependence and brokenness. Acting as both host and guest, the church has a responsibility to make space for the stranger, to accommodate and change. There is also a responsibility to make the Christian story known, but as Michael Barnes underlines, this process involves relationship and cannot be pre-programmed and delineated. Knowing beforehand what you might say or do with the other would undermine the reality of that encounter. If we are not learning as we meet Muslims, we are probably not listening. If Muslims are not learning about the Christian story as they encounter us, we are probably not being fully present.

EN: In your book *Distinctly Welcoming* you have a lovely phrase about God's ways with the world, 'God never colonizes us; he never marches in on us, forcing his ways on our will' (p. 75). What is happening at the Springfield Project is clearly part of God's mission, but how much would you say that it has altered and enriched your previous conceptions of mission?

RS: Surprise has been a frequent outcome of the journey of the Springfield Project: it has not always been possible to anticipate all that might have happened. One elderly member of the congregation who works as a volunteer in the project said, 'I used to pray for the Muslims here as enemies. I now pray for them as friends.' Preparing drinks for local mothers at the Stay-and-Play, she did not expect, when she started, that she would now be talking of friendships with Muslims. For both Christians and Muslims, the Springfield Project has become an arena where mutual encounters have been made possible that bring to light a shared understanding that God is our ultimate host. The impetus for mission has led the church community into its own process of conversion and transformation.

As the Christian staff and volunteers root their public practices in prayer and scripture, Muslims recognize the seriousness of a faith that is intrinsically public. This has freed Muslims to talk of their own spirituality, bringing the 'surprise' of mutual recognition alongside the acknowledgement of strangeness. So, as the Christian volunteers gather to pray before each Stay-and-Play, Muslims are reassured that this is a place that is hallowed before God, though perhaps bemused that no external postures or preconditions are required for prayer.

EN: I am particularly interested in your last point, because it sheds light on a difference between the way Muslims may respond to the evangelical and catholic strands in Anglicanism. Once a week we celebrate the Eucharist in our church community centre. On occasion, I have noticed fascinated glances from passers-by, sometimes on the top deck of a passing bus, as they see the priest genuflecting, robed, before the sacrament on its Gopak altar! Making the sign of the cross is equally intriguing to the little Muslim boy who often accompanies one of our elderly parishioners to the coffee morning in the room next door. While the sacraments and symbolism of catholic worship may be a stumbling block in Christian–Muslim encounters, the use of the body in ritual disciplines and habits may be welcome common ground.

When we were recently approached by a Shia Muslim group wishing to make use of one of the rooms at the centre for Friday prayers, one of the first subjects I raised was the fact that the room in question was used each week for Christian worship. Far from being a problem, it seemed to be part of the attraction that this was a place that reached beyond itself into its source and origin in God.

I think this goes hand in hand with my opening anecdote about the church steps. Places of worship exercise an attraction on a surprisingly wide range of people. When I have tried to tease this out with people, the first thing they tend to mention is the sense of safety and protection – even when shivering in the cold and wet on the back steps. But alongside this is a paradoxical sense of openness that borders on vulnerability. People of a wide range of backgrounds and ages behave differently in and around places of worship. Some of this is just unfamiliarity, but it is also an awareness of something greater than themselves in a building that is evidently more than merely utilitarian. To return to 'Nick', his demeanour when I meet him elsewhere in the parish is friendly, but streetwise and brisk. When I encounter him around the church he is set free from some of this protective carapace, just as I may be, too, if I allow God's grace to release me from the programmed reactions of a professional carer.

I have been accused of undue romanticism for saying this, but the changes that often come over people's bodies in and around church are fascinating. Hardened street faces relax, eyes brighten, hands unclench: it is often as if unbearably burdened bodies, for a brief while at least, may relax and blossom simply through proximity to a place dedicated to the worship of the One whose yoke is easy. Something similar happens with the many school groups who come to St Andrew's. My opening gambit is always to make them *look* and *listen*: to *look* upwards to the roof and imagine themselves on a voyage in an upturned boat; to *listen* to the sound of sheer silence – or as near to it as you can get in postcode B21. It amazes me that this is just as successful with teenagers as with 6 year olds – would that those of us more familiar with these liminal places were so open-minded!

RS: Yes, I agree with you about the appeal of what is seen as 'hallowed' across faiths, and especially to children and young people. I wonder if in my own Anglican evangelical tradition more of the mystery of ritual and liturgy needs to be reclaimed. Interestingly, one of the most powerful community events for the Springfield Project is the Stay-and-Play's annual 'scratch' nativity play. Parents and children love this retelling of the Christmas story when children volunteer on the spot, are dressed in costume and enact the appropriate parts. It is vivid and full of joy, yet never fails to carry a something of genuine spiritual weight across the faiths.

St Christopher's is responding to this tangible sense of hallowed actions and places by returning the church's side chapel into a dedicated prayer space from its recent incarnation as an office! The hope is to create a space for stillness amidst the busyness and activity of the church and children's centre so that people can experience an encounter with God that is beyond our words and efforts.

We need to have integrity here within our respective traditions. Bishop Kenneth Cragg, the great Anglican Islamicist, argues that a proper understanding of our roles as stewards of creation provides a platform for public life that we can share, despite our differences. Cragg sees a parallel between the biblical mandate of human 'dominion' in accountability to a creator God and Surah 2:30 of the Qur'an: 'I am appointing a viceroy in the earth.' The Qur'anic concept of the *khalifah*, (the role of 'viceroy', or 'caliph', designated to each and every human) asserts the privilege of humanity over the earth but *for* God. This is an inclusive mandate to all humanity that demonstrates a divine restraint. There is a risk in the heart of God, as God delegates the ordering of social life over a good creation. This risk is not always readily apparent in typically Islamic accounts, but can be found in Surah 2, as the angels demur at such delegation. What Kenneth Cragg offers us is a theological basis for finding common ground between Christians and Muslims.

Cragg's understanding is certainly helpful for Anglican Christians engaging with Muslims. The Church of England takes seriously its 'cure of souls', or responsibility for all people in the parish. This means that no person or place is beyond the purview of the church: our stewardship before God does not permit a sectarian withdrawal from the concerns of wider society. Anglicans look back to the theologian Richard Hooker who developed an Anglican polity that could witness to a realm that was *properly* 'secular', that is, of the saeculum, the time between the first and second coming of Christ. The inherent sociality of humanity, for Hooker, meant that shared deliberations around the common good could justify the temporal sovereignty of the crown, for example. His Puritan detractors sought to order social arrangements through explicit biblical precedent alone, but Hooker argued effectively for the delegated responsibility of humanity in public life. Cragg is influenced by this: God's providence is evinced in nature and in the sociality of humanity, and we should not be perturbed to find solutions to the common good that encompass faith, tradition *and* reason. So what makes a good city, school, hospital or political system concerns us all. These shared goods demand a shared deliberation and, in pushing our horizons beyond the limits of 'self' and the confines of our own community, move us to consider the true author of the good.

EN: Hooker is, I agree, a rich resource. I think his greatest gift to the contemporary Church of England is the centrality he accords to participation: God's share in us and ours in God, despite the encumbrances of sin. Hooker sees that the gospel call is not just to imitate Christ, but to share in him. 'What would Jesus do?' is a good question, but better still is to challenge myself to behave mindful of the fact that I am in Christ and he is in me – and, moreover, that he is in the stranger and neighbour I am engaging or ignoring. Hooker gives the doctrine of participation a firm christological grounding. For him, Christ is the source, opening a path that enables us all to relate to one another as God relates to us; but Christ is also the goal, to whom we shall be conformed, body and soul, in glory.

One of the more hopeful signs of change in the contemporary ecumenical scene in Handsworth is the increasing willingness of the Pentecostal and Charismatic churches to engage in the public square. This is partly a function of numerical strength and growing confidence, but it is also due to a new recognition of the public realm as a field for mission. It is remarkable that the larger

Pentecostal churches no longer see mission as purely about the conversion of the lost, but as about corporate engagement in the full range of local life, from street pastors to carol services and cultural awareness initiatives.

It has been said that in any encounter between two human beings four people are present: you and I, but also your image of me and mine of you. Miroslav Volf – a Pentecostal turned Anglican – has refined this model, writing of the involvement of *seven* in situations of true dialogue. To the four he adds 'my image of myself (which may not be true to who I am and may be very much *un*like who *you* think I am)' and 'your image of yourself (which may not be true to who you are and may be very much *un*like who *I* think you are)'; the seventh is God, the absolutely truthful and infinitely merciful One... who demands our truthful self-perception as well as the truthful perceiving of others'. 'Indeed,' he adds, 'God desires of us to be *as* truthful and *as* merciful with ourselves, with one another, and with the world as he is truthful and merciful.'

It is not fanciful, I believe, to see this perspective on dialogue as stemming from the same sources as the two aspects of Hooker's thought we have identified: delegated responsibility and participation. God does not dictate the shape that our relationships with our fellow human beings should take, but leaves us to negotiate them with truthfulness and mercy: this is our delegated responsibility. But the very act of faithfully exercising this responsibility invites us to participate in the nature of God. This is one of those crucial areas in which the theory and practice of theology meet.

RS: I agree. Recognizing the church as a vital sacrament in a sacramental universe is where that reading of Hooker and Volf takes us! We participate in the triune God that goes beyond our borders: what the Church Fathers term the ecstatic of God.

The shared 'dominion' was vividly realized when planning permission was being sought for the Springfield Project children's centre building. A city councillor was disturbed that significant public sector funds were going to a church building in a Muslim-majority ward. Then the neighbouring mosque wrote a letter, countering the political opportunism of the local councillor and supporting the development on behalf of the church. For the mosque leadership, the Springfield Project made a positive difference to the common good, transformed the lives of families, particularly among their own Muslim community, and so they were happy to encourage it. The mosque demonstrated our shared public concern, rooted in our responsibility to God. They also exemplified the fluidity of the host–guest relationship that I mentioned before: the church was dependent upon the mosque; the mosque was dependent upon the church.

Where there is a concern for shared goods – in our case, for the welfare of young families in the Springfield parish – then many different communities and associations will be involved in the deliberation. For St Christopher's and the Springfield Project, the vital third party has been Birmingham City Council. The council had a mandate to build children's centres. It would have been easy to have been ambivalent; indeed many at St Christopher's and the mosque were. Was it a genuinely shared good – or just about funding projects in order to tick boxes? How could we know if this was really about grassroots transformation? We thought that if the council responded positively, and acknowledged the Christian inspiration for the Springfield Project and the goal to serve Muslim families inclusively, then the council might well be on board. We needed to show that there was a shared deliberation across church, mosque, council and community, putting into practice what Rowan Williams has described as 'interactive pluralism': the inclusive human task bridging acknowledged differences of tradition. So the Springfield Project made clear its Christian roots and values to the council. They were not put off, and they have seen how the Christian faith has brought an inclusive service in a multi-faith area.

Throughout the life of the Springfield Project, there has never been a deliberate policy to seek public sector funding or employ Muslim staff. These things have simply happened as shared concerns for the common good have developed, often within the cut and thrust of different relationships and all the discovery, surprise, learning and challenge that goes with them. We have seen how the language of the city council has become more attuned to faith – due partly to the robustness of the Islamic understanding of public life. Councils are having to adapt. The mosque communities have learned the language of statutory provision. Such changes are often because the Anglican Church acts as a broker in a society that hasn't quite forgotten what a vicar is. Working for the common good has affirmed the interdependency of church and mosque, and in turn, statutory services. In what is clearly a complex set of relationships, St Christopher's, through the Springfield Project, has been a significant element as both host and guest.

EN: Would you agree that many, if not most, faithful Christians tend to approach people of other faiths with some anxiety: fearful of causing offence or being offended, suspicious of others' motivation (or their own)? How far has that been the case with the Springfield Project and what has happened on the way to dispel it?

RS: To begin with, there was a very clear trajectory of mission for the Springfield Project: from the church to the Muslim community; providing *for* and proclaiming *to*. But as the church came to understand the Christian's encounter with the Muslim other as both challenge and challenging, that view of mission has changed. If Muslims can be friends as well as clients, colleagues as well as service-users, then what is God doing in our community, and how must we join? We have already noted the growing acknowledgment of the shared goods between Christians and Muslims. Now we understand God's mission to be about families and young children, and changing lives, which are goals wanted by church and community alike. There has been a shift towards much greater partnership and cooperation. Muslims now bring their ideas and leadership into the Springfield Project. We now work together as friends.

Some years ago, there was a notable Springfield Project summer party when church members were encouraged to offer Christian prayer for members of the local community. A Muslim parent, so impressed by the answer to prayer she received, wished to join a midweek prayer meeting at the church. The initial response from church members was discomfort. 'Perhaps she might like to arrange an appointment to pray with the vicar?' This Muslim woman's retort was, 'Isn't it more powerful when a large group meet together for prayer?' A confident and transparent Christian spirituality within the community project had released spiritual confidence in a Muslim which then challenged the fears among the Christians. We, too, were learning.

There has been much to learn. Turning to Kenneth Cragg again, only under God can true dominion be realized, and any human endeavour will always be provisional. We have to accept the temporal nature of projects, politics, the state, and even church institutions. It is a sobering reminder to the Church of England, as an established church with declining resources, that its mission is always penultimate. Thus we have faced the question about whether the city council would swamp the project once the children's centre was built. Or would the developing demography of the city bequeath a state-of-the-art children's centre to Muslim ownership in years to come? Would the employment of Muslims compromise the Christian values of the Springfield Project? These, and many other questions, have been asked and remain unanswered with any certainty. There are many perfectly rational reasons for the church community to be fearful about its long-term status in the city. However, the relationships of hospitality that I have outlined have actually meant that risks have been taken in generosity, and the church has not held all the cards in advance. In so doing, we have been blessed in unexpected ways, and from unexpected quarters. We, too, have found the blessing of your visitor Nick, giving to us far more than we have given. It has felt like a risk, often in the midst of fear. It has meant a pouring out of ourselves in the hope that peace and reconciliation would replace our anxieties.

EN: As the Established Church we are in a position to take risks that others might not hazard. Of course, we are also sometimes

hidebound, sclerotic and complacent, but our residual place in the fabric of national life can be a blessing. As Grace Davie has observed, a 'weak state church' is well placed to negotiate a path between secular relativism and the fundamentalism of 'furious religion'. I am very conscious of the sensitivities in discussing an ongoing project, but I wonder if you could share something of the risks taken at Springfield, perhaps especially those that have not readily borne fruit?

RS: So much remains fragile. What we're doing is not universally shared within the congregation. For some, Muslims remain 'competitors' and the political sensitivities that surround Christian–Muslim relations mean that the goodwill that has been built up over the years could easily be destroyed at a stroke. Furthermore, the church has so far failed to foster sufficient trust with our neighbouring mosque, and a formalized partnership to employ a community youth worker jointly remains unlikely. The deep needs within the community, and dysfunctional practices and perceptions across our various religious and cultural groups, continue to demand more collaborative responses. We are highly conscious that the quality of our relationships will see us through the difficult times, and the political visibility of Islam makes the likelihood of threats to good relations very likely. There can be no let-up in the maintenance of the structural relations with mosque and community leadership, yet, ironically, the growing 'success' in church and project often seems to constrain the time and attention needed to maintain a strong relational presence.

Grace Davie's expression of the 'weak state church' raises all sorts of issues. The church needs to retain its integrity and witness to the weakness of the cross even when it is locally powerful. When it does remain true to the cross, the church can offer a challenge to the classic Islamic aspiration of political power as the ultimate end of religious piety. The ambiguity of this for Anglican Christians means that we need always to oppose the temptation of privilege with the truth of the cross. At the Eucharist the church comes, in repentance, to a cross that measures the failings of a humanity that can only be redeemed in Christ.

For St Christopher's, the journey into a humbling and mutually dependent relationship with the Muslim communities around us has not meant that we have denied the need to proclaim Christ as crucial to the life and worship of the church. Rather, this proclamation has itself become more relevant as the Christian story has become patterned in a community given over in love and service, always challenged by the cross not to be self-seeking, manipulative or powerful in worldly ways. Both the Christian and Muslim faiths make universal claims, and this has been made explicit. The neighbouring mosque community has made direct challenges to church leaders concerning the claims of the Islamic faith. In turn, invitations have been made to mosque leaders to courses introducing the Christian faith. Established relationships are not ignoring crucial divergences between the faiths, but instead they are creating confidence that these can be made transparent without compromising friendship, shared goals and the integrities of our traditions.

EN: One of the plans of the Parochial Church Council at St Andrew's is to make our sports and community centre more of a visible Christian hub for the parish. Within our walls the most astonishing juxtapositions take place: as a Shia Muslim group packs up after Friday prayers, a West African charismatic church begins praying in tongues next door; and everything from Tai Chi to bereavement counselling and lace-making may be taking place elsewhere. There is less overlap than there might be between these different users of our halls, but much of this rich mixture is and has been enabled by the faithful witness, unassertive but confident, of our church and its parishioners over recent decades. What we need to work on is realizing and articulating what is already happening and then making plain its Christian origins. I know that much the same could be said of the day-to-day life of the Springfield Project and I wonder if some of its habits and practices might have a wider application.

RS: Each term we have a day away for staff and volunteers. This training day brings together people who are Christian, Muslim, and of other faiths – all those who share the tasks under the umbrella of the Springfield Project. A vital discipline has been developed that affirms the Christian values of the Springfield Project, reminding everyone what has birthed and sustained the work. This is done in a way that makes clear connections with daily practices constitutive of good care or working as a team. For example, the head of centre may wish to talk about positive working relationships – that if there are issues among staff and volunteers, these are resolved without gossip or back-biting. This would be reaffirmed by reference to Christian teaching, in this case, the Christian imperative to forgive, as a mandate given by Jesus. Then the floor is opened for staff and volunteers to share their faith inspiration for the behaviours ('shared goods') that are being acknowledged and encouraged. So, what may follow is a parable of Muhammad about how we should not bear grudges. The church, through the Springfield Project, hosts and enables such reciprocal faith-sharing, becoming vulnerable to the risk of receiving and hearing challenges to itself from another faith. This, I believe, is a model that could well be adapted to similar contexts elsewhere.

EN: Throughout our discussion there has been a real sense of gratitude for what your Muslim context in Springfield has enabled among the Christian community at St Christopher's. The barriers against 'doing God' tend to be much lower in areas with a strong presence of other religions. The heart of the matter is our motivation: why are we doing this? If the answer is anything less than to share the generous, open-handed, unconditional love of God, there is something amiss.

Yet, as with most such endeavours, there are paradoxes in what is happening: a renewal of Christian worship that has allowed the freedom to relate to Muslim neighbours; the value of mission, and even evangelism, as positive forces in Muslim–Christian relations; the particular power relations in Springfield, where Islam is dominant in numbers but feels under political scrutiny and is relatively impoverished and Anglicanism can afford to be generous as the established church.

RS: For St Christopher's, the experiences of the Springfield Project are essentially about a Christian faith increasingly lived in the public square, amidst the push and pull of genuine diversity. Though there are particular characteristics of the Muslim faith that provide a special challenge to faith lived 'in public', the lessons of being both host and guest are surely relevant to any British context. The 'other' may be a town council suspicious of religion, an unchurched estate or a community of urban spiritual seekers; but the mission of the Church of England assumes that the abundance we have found in Christ can make a difference to, and indeed find resonances beyond, the borders of our rites of worship. At St Christopher's, this journey has led the church to risk itself – but it has received so much in return. I would suggest that there is a lesson of confidence here for the Church of England as it faces an uncertain future in our inner cities.[1]

The Revd Richard J. Sudworth is pioneer curate to Christ Church, Sparkbrook, and St Edmund's Tyseley, Birmingham. He was formerly chair of the Springfield Project and a Church Mission Society mission partner in Birmingham and North Africa. He is a doctoral candidate at Heythrop College, University of London.

The Revd Dr Edmund Newey is vicar of St Andrew's, Handsworth.

Note

1   The principles Richard outlines here are more fully explored in his book *Distinctly Welcoming: Christian Presence in a Multifaith Society* (Bletchley: Scripture Union, 2007). Kenneth Cragg's seminal work, *The Call of the Minaret* (Oxford: Oxford University Press, 1964), remains the towering Anglican response to Islam, and his book *The Privilege of Man: A Theme in Judaism, Islam and Christianity* (London: The Athlone Press, 1968), outlines his thoughts on the shared dominion of humanity. Michael Barnes' *Theology and the Dialogue of Religions* (Cambridge: Cambridge University Press, 2002) has been an invaluable text for inter-religious dialogue that can account for difference and commonality. *Generous Love: The Truth of the Gospel and the Call to Dialogue*, is a significant contemporary resource describing the particular gift of Anglicanism to relations with other faiths and can be downloaded from: http://nifcon.anglicancommunion.org/resources/documents/generous_love.cfm. The quotation from Rowan Williams is taken from 'Theological Resources for Re-examining Church' in Steven Croft (ed.),

The Future of the Parish System: Shaping the Church of England for the 21st Century (London: Church House Publishing, 2006). The quotation from Miroslav Volf is from Miroslav Volf, Ghazi bin Muhammad and Melissa Yarrington (eds), *A Common Word: Muslims and Christians on Loving God and Neighbour* (Grand Rapids: Eerdmans, 2010).

From Portsmouth and Birmingham we now turn to Bradford for the next four chapters. The impetus for this volume grew out of the reflections of Canon Frances Ward as she thought about her work at the cathedral in Bradford, particularly with Muslim women in the city. What follows gives a series of snapshots of that engagement from various people she got to know there. Philip Lewis is a leading international expert on Islam who lives in Bradford. In many respects his contribution is a key introduction to some of the dynamic challenges and currents to be found as Muslim-heritage people make their home in Britain.

The next contribution in this section comes from Nuzhat Ali, who writes as a Muslim woman who has lived in Bradford since she was brought there as a young child from Pakistan. Since adulthood she has embraced the Muslim faith, believing that it brings much good to British society when it is allowed to contribute to public life. She is a leading member of the Islamic Society of Britain, an organization that holds together a positive understanding of the good of British society with a serious practice of faith.[1] With Faiths in Action funding from the government, from 2008 to 2010 Nuzhat worked alongside Frances Ward and others at Bradford Cathedral, modelling the public practice of friendship that allowed difficult issues and topics to be addressed. Here she reflects in depth on the nature of Islamophobia, with an appreciation of how distorting it can be as it shapes people's lives.

Then Frances describes her own experience. She moved to Bradford in 2006 from north Manchester, with a desire to learn more, aware that her Anglican traditions and practice were insufficient to give her the resources to understand and engage properly with the different Muslim communities that were growing around her. What would it be like to remain true to Christ and commend Christ by seeking to develop friendships of such quality that they could bear a proper and true engagement with some of the more difficult areas of difference?

After a couple of years in post as a residentiary canon at Bradford Cathedral, Frances was approached by Imran Manzoor. He had experienced how seductive ideological Islam could be and believed that the best way to give young people – of any background – the resources to stave off the attractions of extremist ideologies was to encourage them to understand and engage more deeply in the political processes of Western democracy and human rights. He and his team at Via Media believed that violent extremism is born of political ignorance and a form of technocratic politics that does not inspire young people to participate politically. The Via Media team argues that many of the policies of the government have had a detrimental effect by eroding trust and friendship in society. Sitting around the kitchen table, Manzoor and Frances agreed that it would be a good thing if Bradford Cathedral were to host one of the twelve courses a year that Manzoor and his colleagues ran for young people aged 16–21. Manzoor recognized the role of the cathedral – and another Christian church in Bradford called Emerge – as being able to offer active hosting, thereby strengthening trust and friendship in society and countering fear and violence. He raises many of the issues that face social and political initiatives which are concerned to enhance civil resilience and promote social cohesion and the double-bind in which they can find themselves: funded and scrutinized simultaneously. Many aspects of government policy betray a profound ignorance and fear, and when this turns into conflicting messages, the trust so necessary to a healthy society becomes quickly eroded. This chapter has important things to contribute to the debates about the Big Society. The course and the ideas behind it are described here, at a time when Manzoor and his two colleagues Miriam Mushayi and Javaad Alipoor faced the withdrawal of their funding and so the end of the project. The approach here is somewhat different to the other contributions of the book because it steps back to reflect as the course faced closure.

3

From Identity Politics to Engagement: Making Sense of Muslim Communities in Britain

Philip Lewis

In this chapter Philip Lewis maps the diversity in background, tradition, history and ethnicity for Britain's Muslims. He looks at the variety of Muslim communities in different areas of Britain and the variation in class status and education across those communities. He discusses ways in which British Muslims are adjusting – or not – to a problematic minority status against an historically supersessionist theological tradition; the issue of the training and outlook of imams in Britain; and the uneasy and traumatic impact of 7/7 and the 'war on terror'.

Introduction

Readers of this book with little direct knowledge of the Muslim communities in Britain will be exposed to a variety of unfamiliar names which denote 'schools of thought' in contemporary Islam, such as the following: Salafi and Sufi, Islamist and traditionalist, Deobandi and Barelwi. To British Muslims these are as familiar as the labels contemplative and Calvinist, Catholic and Protestant, Orthodox and Pentecostal are to Christians. This chapter seeks to provide a preliminary map to help the uninitiated make sense of both this variety and the complex dynamics of development within the

Muslim communities. Historically, Islam has been embedded in five distinct geographical and linguistic worlds as the majority religion: Arab, Turkic, South East Asia, South Asia and parts of Africa, as well as a minority presence in many other parts of the world.

The last 50 years have seen Muslims migrate from many of these areas to establish a new and significant presence in Britain, Western Europe and North America. Muslims and western societies have not found this easy, especially since 11 September 2001 and 7 July 2005. However, one far-sighted historian of Christianity and Christian–Muslim relations argues that in the long term this could be significant for both Muslims and Christians alike: if Muslims are to be at ease in Western Europe they will have to quarry the riches of their own inherited religious traditions to engage with both democracy and religious pluralism in a principled way. Similarly, Christians will have to explore the variety of their own ecumenical traditions to relate to such Muslim diversity. Indeed, the same historian hints that Muslim communities in the West could be vehicles of Christian renewal.[2] The essays in this collection suggest that such hopes are not delusional.

No one is a Muslim-in-general
Muslim communities carry radically different histories and diverse cultural baggage with them into Britain. There are some 100,000 Muslims from Turkish backgrounds in London: they have little public profile and seldom feature among the faces of angry young radicals protesting against issues frequently portrayed by the media. As a people the Turks were never colonized; indeed, they were the colonizers and creators of the Ottoman Empire, which included much of the Arab world and parts of southern Europe. Further, they have had more than 70 years of uncompromising, doctrinaire secularism which Ataturk borrowed from the French. Finally, many define themselves as European: Turkey is part of NATO and wants to join the European Union.

This stands in marked contrast to many Muslims from South Asia, who according to the 2001 census comprised about 70 per cent of the 1.6 million British Muslims. These figures are approximate, but roughly 42 per cent of this group have roots in Pakistan, 17 per cent in Bangladesh and 7 per cent in India. South Asia was colonized by the British. The majority communities come from Pakistan and they hold that British policy has invariably favoured India. They are often referred to as 'the new Irish'. Like the Irish, Pakistanis also carried into Britain negative stereotypes of the British. This is evident in the content and ethos of specific, imported religious traditions, as will become clear later when we consider the world of the imams in the mosques.

Algerians, Egyptians and Saudis – from whom were drawn the 'Arab Afghans' who comprise the backbone of al-Qaeda – have never been numerically significant in Britain. Most Arabs in London either fall into the category of international commuters – London has been dubbed 'Beirut-on-Thames' by journalists – or they are well educated students who have chosen to stay. Another portion of this group is in political exile, and their focus remains on their home country.[3]

Ethno-religious clustering and the socio-economic profile of Muslims in Britain

Notwithstanding the ethnic diversity of Muslim communities in Britain, it is Pakistanis who tend to shape the public profile of Islam. Seventy per cent of Pakistanis are from Azad Kashmir, one of the least developed areas in Pakistan. Their traditionalism is kept alive by a constant and sustained flow of religious leaders, politicians, investment and high levels of transcontinental marriages. Just over half of the Muslim communities are under 25, as compared to one third in wider society. Since the average number of children in Pakistani and Bangladeshi families is almost twice the national figure, this suggests that ethno-Muslim communities could almost double within the next 20 years.[4]

If Muslims are to be incorporated equitably into British society, policy makers will have to focus on cities, for it is there that Muslims are disproportionately concentrated. I am speaking here of those cities, especially in the North, where the industries which attracted migrant labour have collapsed. Since most young Muslims are from

'a working-class culture with the majority ... living in neighbourhoods considered to be the most deprived wards in England ... [this
is] reflected in statistics as underachievers, anti-school rather than
pro-school and generally displaying signs of disengagement with
school authorities'.[5] Despite narrowing the educational gap in the
last few years, as other communities have done, the gap between
male and female success remains wide. Furthermore, 35 per cent
of Muslim families are growing up within households where no
adult is in employment (the national figure is 17 per cent) and
unemployment levels are three times the national figure. 68 per cent
of Muslim women are economically inactive, as compared to less
than 30 per cent for Christian women and approximately 35 per cent
for Hindu and Sikh women.[6]

Class and cultural differences, in part, explain some educational
and employment differentials across the different Muslim communities. An historian of Muslims in Britain notes:

> Not only was a higher proportion (75.4 %) of men from the
> Middle Eastern, predominantly Muslim, groups more economi-
> cally active than white males, but the percentage of economically
> participating females from this group was higher than for their
> white counterparts ... Local variations have been striking.
> According to the 1991 census, while 11.8 % of Bangladeshis
> were unemployed in Brent, a colossal 47.3 % were out of work
> in Tower Hamlets.[7]

Brent is not Leicester is not Bradford

Different cities have quite distinct profiles: Brent is one of the most
ethnically diverse Muslim communities in UK. It is the place to
which the upwardly mobile British Bengalis move from Tower
Hamlets. A recent localized study indicates that there are some 30
ethnic groups in Brent.[8] This ethnic diversity has generated huge
creativity, as Brent is the home of Islamic Human Rights groups,
pioneering Muslim women's groups – An-Nisa – and the home of

British Muslim magazines in English, whether *Q-News* or *Emel*. Further north, in the East Midlands, a majority of Leicester's Muslim communities are 'twice migrants', with origins in East Africa. They fled brutal Africanization under Idi Amin, and arrived with considerable 'cultural capital'. They had learned to live as a minority in East Africa over the previous 50 years; they were English speakers and had generated commercial and professional networks. They have contributed greatly to the local economy.[9]

It is from such communities of Brent and Leicester that the YUMMIE phenomenon has emerged: Young Upwardly Mobile Muslims who provide a market for the beautifully produced Muslim lifestyle magazines, such as *Emel*. From this group other activist Muslim groups are drawn: young professionals who have pioneered the City Circle, for example. This is a space in London where Muslims working in the city can debate what it means to be a British Muslim. There are also the young adults in their 20s who created the Muslim Youth Helpline which is a counselling service providing an institutional arena where issues of sexuality, relationship and mental health can be discussed. These are issues which are frequently taboo among elders and religious leaders, and so to claim such an established service is significant. The YUMMIE phenomenon also provides the 17–25 year olds whom the previous government identified as a 'critical friend' for policy makers, as exemplified by the Young Muslim Advisory Group (YMAG)[10].

In contrast to Brent and Leicester, Bradford – like many northern cities – has suffered massive de-industrialization with high levels of unemployment. Some 60,000 textile jobs were lost between 1960 and 1990. The majority of the city's growing Muslim communities have roots in rural Kashmir, and they are very young communities: in the 2001 census, 16 per cent of the population had roots in Pakistan and Bangladesh, but accounted for 28 per cent of the school population.

The Pakistani communities include a growing 'underclass', with a significant section of young men underachieving in schools and joining an intractable white underclass on outer estates. This opens the door to extremists in both communities intent on capitalizing on a widespread feeling of malaise, whether the BNP or Hizb ut-Tahrir [HT], 'the Party of Liberation', a radical Islamist movement with roots in Palestine.[11] Both are carriers of a supremacist ideology, one based on a selective interpretation of 'Englishness', the other an equally tendentious interpretation of Islam. Little wonder one of our Muslim essayists wearies at the disproportionate media profile enjoyed by Anjem Chaudhry, who is a leader of one of the small splinter groups of HT. Alas, he also belongs to the YUMMIES!

Youth alienation amongst sections of British 'Pakistani' and white communities translates into major problems with crime, drugs and antisocial behaviour. The prison population now includes a disproportionate 'Muslim' component[12] and high crime rates accelerate the flight of the affluent away from Muslim communities and can threaten the stability required for businesses to flourish, and inward investment. Relations between British Pakistanis and English communities are rendered difficult by a number of factors: a measure of residential segregation, which is even more apparent in schools that have become ever more ethnically homogeneous; and high levels of youth unemployment, which means there is little interaction at work. This means that all too often, there are neither opportunities, institutional spaces nor a common vocabulary to talk openly and honestly about problems within and between communities. There is a fear of being labelled racist if wrongdoing is challenged, a fear of confronting the gang culture, the illegal drugs trade and growing intolerance, harassment, domestic abuse and 'forced marriages'[13].

Identity and belonging: not easy being Muslim after 7/7

In the 1990s there was a new emphasis by British Muslims on 'identity politics'. Muslim identity politics was apiece with multiculturalism and the pluralization of interest groups, whether the basis was race, gender, sexuality or regional. Where one could argue that one's identity needed recognition, resources and representation followed. As one acute social scientist noticed, Muslim identity becomes integral to local community politics and yet thrives through romantic, global solidarities as wars and massacres in Palestine, Bosnia, Kosovo, the Gulf, Chechnya, Kashmir, India and so on fill our newspapers and television screens and lead some young, British-born Muslims to reinvent the concept of the *umma*, the global community of Muslims, as global victims.[14]

Such politics persisted in the new millennium with Afghanistan and Iraq adding to the list of grievances. While educated Muslims would organize aid to stricken areas or join radical groups, most young men among working class Muslims in the inner cities did not involve themselves in Muslim organizations. Instead, they used Islam in the construction of an assertive identity which was little more than a tribal badge.[15]

There is a satisfying and seductive allure about representing oneself as a victim. It relieves communities from self-criticism. However, this was less easy after 7 July 2005, which was a shock for Muslim and non-Muslim alike. The fact that British Muslims had visited such an atrocity on their fellow citizens began a period of soul searching in sections of the Muslim community, as shown by many of the contributors to this volume. However, it also opened Muslim communities to intense and sustained scrutiny, whether from the media, politicians, academics or intelligence services. Hardly any aspect of community life has been spared the unwelcome glare of media attention: specific cultural practices and abuses have been conflated with Islam, everything from 'forced marriages', female genital mutilation, head scarves and face coverings – hijab and niqab – to gun crime, gangs and heroin distribution. Moreover, stoning for adultery and amputations for theft, as practised by Saudis and the Taliban, are presented as normative for all Muslims in all places for all time. An understandable weariness with such a barrage of negative media depiction has generated debate around the extent to which 'Islamophobia' exists in British society.[16]

Many educated Muslims have begun a process of self-education, tapping into 'Shaykh Google' to find answers to the many questions a sceptical society is now asking about Islam. This can have both liberating and disturbing consequences. British Muslim women are finding their voice and beginning

> ... to question the elders by comparing what they had discovered in the sources of Islam with what their elders believed. This situation occurs in a range of issues from forced marriages to seeking higher education ... females [are] particularly vociferous in discussing the topic of education ... They argued that their parents' expectations of them and what they understood as their rights and responsibilities as a Muslim were, at times, at polar opposites ... [This can generate] constant battles about topical issues or leading double lives.[17]

Young women are especially agitated by the importation from the parental homeland of the *biraderi* (literarily 'brotherhood') system (traditional Indo-Pakistani tribal system of social order) in which kinship and age are important. The traditional tribal hierarchical system is criticized by many young Muslims; they argue that respect and honour should be gained through diligence and hard work and not given because someone is older or of high ranking in the caste system.[18] These clan networks, at once patriarchal and hierarchical, impact on many aspects of Pakistani communities: mosques, community centres and local politics are often the preserve of such 'clans'. Because there is a pecking order of such 'brotherhoods', the more influential and numerous embody a pattern of exclusionary politics. Yet local party bosses often find it convenient to work with such clans because they can guarantee vote banks.[19]

For many young Muslim men living in the inner city there has been a process of multiple alienations, from wider society, mosque and home. Three vivid quotations communicate some of the reasons for the alienation of many young men in northern towns from mosque and home alike. 'Basid' speaks to a young Muslim researcher about the attitudes of wider society:

Oh, they're a bunch of wankers, yeah? They keep telling us to sod off. I don't know if there's a single day that I don't hear 'Paki go home,' ... They don't get that I was born here, I've lived here all my life. I've only been to Pakistan twice in my life cuz of a wedding and my daadi's died. I'm gonna live here ... and I'll probably die here too.

A 22-year-old man, 'Jaleel', in reply to a question about mosques expostulates:

Who goes to the mosque, mate? Do you? The mullah don't speak our language, yeah? They [the elders comprising the mosque committee] bring some f***ing villager over here and he gets up there and tells us every Friday that we are shite and we're a bunch of wankers and we chase birds all day long and we aren't good Muslims. Who needs it man? I know my shit ... I know how to live in the UK. That f***er hasn't been here for more than a few years and he thinks he knows where it's at ...

Similarly, for many British Muslim youth, their homes are also unsympathetic places. 'Ashfaq' comments that:

Me mum loves PTV [Pakistan Television] shite, man. She watch [sic] it all day long. All I get at home is what some f***er is doing in Lahore or Multan or some shite village ... I got to call me mates to get the footie scores, man, cuz I don't get no telly time at home. I mean, I don't care f*** all what's going on in some shite village in that shite country. I wanna know what's outside my door; me mum's only caring about what's happening over there ...[20]

Such young men seek sanctuary with their 'mates' on the streets. A perceptive Muslim thinker and social psychologist refers to these young men as 'rude boys', the products of three cultures:

'African-American hip hop, Northern Pakistani and Northern Industrial'. This phenomenon reflects social changes in British society – 'the rise of excessive individualism, detraditionalisation, demoralisation or the "hollowing out" of modern society'. When such young men embrace Islam it is as if 'they have found religion but not become religious. The Islam ... offered [to them] is the Islam of outer semblances that replicates so well the cultural commodification that they exhibited as rude boys'.[21]

Specific intellectual challenges facing Muslims as a minority

Thus far, I have concentrated on social issues and patterns of exclusion that British Muslims face, both internal and external. This is important because many young Muslims, especially in the inner city, face similar problems to white working class lads: poor education, impoverished environment, high levels of unemployment – a situation in which young men, 'hoodies', become the new folk devils.

However, British Muslims, beyond the need to make a multiplicity of practical accommodations to a culture and society very different to that which their parents or grandparents left behind, also face a new set of intellectual tasks posed by being a minority in Western society. Islamic jurisprudence (*fiqh*) did not envisage minority Muslim communities formed by voluntary economic migration from Muslim to non-Muslim lands. Over a quarter of a century ago, the late Sheikh Dr Zaki Badawi (d. 2006) lamented the fact that Sunni 'Muslim theology offers, up to the present, no systematic formulation of the status of being in a minority'.[22]

An Indian scholar also observes that with the exception of the recent trauma of Western colonialism, 'Sunni Muslims took power and dominance for granted. They knew how to command or to obey. They had, for most of their history, rarely learned to live with others in equality and fraternity'.[23] He was so concerned with the lack of critical thinking in a world in which one in five Muslims now live as minorities that he created the *Journal for Muslim Minority Affairs*.

Nor are Muslims better equipped for interfaith relations with

Christians. One of the few British Muslim scholars who has actually studied Christianity regrets that 'a frank supersessionism written into the Islamic tradition leaves little need for "curiosity" about "the otherness of the other"'[24]. This has created a huge hole in Islamic training. Where Muslim scholars, especially those tasked with giving legal answers – the mufti – are required to have some basic knowledge of the local customs and practices of the people amongst whom they live, he notes that:

> In Europe, I am not aware of any *madrasa* which is in the business of training *ulama* [in] even the basic concepts and ideas about the Judaeo-Christian traditions … Furthermore, there is an urgent need to introduce the intellectual and cultural trends of Western society into Muslim seminaries' syllabi.[25]

Living in a society in which Muslims are a minority requires some intellectual developments. One would require Muslims to study the humanities and the social sciences. Unfortunately, most 'young Muslim activists pursue careers in the technical, scientific, medical, financial or legal professions … such career choices of our best and brightest means that we remain culturally delinquent and are unable to recognize the subtleties required for the art of persuasion.'[26] The second requires investment in religious institutions that can generate new thinking. A South African scholar, now in America, has identified with unparalleled clarity the enormity of the challenge this poses:

> The body of thought that the project of re-thinking … attempts to confront is premised on a triumphalist ideology: an age when Islam was a political entity and an empire. A cursory glance at this intellectual legacy will show how this ideology of Empire permeates theology, jurisprudence, ethics, and espouses a worldview that advances hierarchy. What adds to the frustration of millions of followers of Islam is the fact that this triumphalist

creed and worldview is unable to deliver its adherents to its
perceived goals of worldly success and leadership.[27]

In conversation, the same scholar told me that he was working on
a book with the poignant title 'After Empire'. In this work, he seeks
to disengage the religious disciplines from the imperial narrative in
which they are embedded, since that narrative is now dysfunctional.

The world of the mosques and Islamic training

Since more than 70 per cent of British Muslims have roots in
South Asia, the majority of mosques in the United Kingdom have
been created to serve these communities. The most comprehensive
mapping of Britain's mosques with regard to location, ethnicity and
the 'school of thought' to which they belong, suggest that 600 are
Deobandi, 550 Barelwi, 60 Islamists, 75 Salafi, 65 Shi'ite, along with
a number of ethnic-specific mosques serving Turks, Somalis, Arabs
and so on.[28] In short, most reflect the different traditional 'Sunni
schools of thought' active in South Asia – especially Deobandi and
Barelwi. While British Deobandis with roots in India tend to belong
to a pious and a-political tradition, some with roots in Pakistan are
the same ethnic group that has generated the Taliban. Barelwis have
suffered from the 'Talibanization' of Pakistan and, unsurprisingly, are
bitterly hostile to them.

In Britain, most of the mosque committees are dominated by
the elders, whose experiences in rural and small town Pakistan
continue to shape a limited set of expectations about the imam's
status and role. Most are paid well below the minimum wage and
lack contractual security. Their roles are generally confined to the
mosque where they are to lead the five daily prayers, teach children
after state school, give the Friday address, preside over the 'rites of
passage', and offer advice, when sought, within their competence on
the application of Islamic teaching and law.

In the last quarter of a century, a new phase of institution
building has begun with the proliferation of Dar al-'Uloom, 'Islamic
seminaries'. There are at least 24 registered 'seminaries' in Britain:

sixteen Deobandi, five Barelwi, one Shi'ite, one Muslim Brotherhood and one founded by the late Sheikh Dr Zaki Badawi, who trained at Al-Azhar University in Cairo.[29] Many mosque committees still seem reluctant to employ such British-influenced imams – perhaps because they press for realistic salaries, contracts and pension rights. A survey of 300 mosques in 2008 indicated that 92 per cent of the imams were foreign born and trained, and only 6 per cent speak English as their first language. This creates a significant disconnect between many mosques and the 52 per cent of British Muslims under 25 years old, most of whom are British-born and British-educated.[30]

The ethos of South Asian 'seminaries', from which the majority of such imams come, can still be characterized as rejectionist of modernity and of discourses developed outside its circumscribed world. A recent survey of Pakistani students studying at Urdu and (elite) English medium schools and universities, public and private, registered between 65 and 90 per cent across the different institutions as favouring equal rights for women. This stands in marked contrast with 'seminarians', for whom the figure was 17 per cent. Significant differences were also evident with regard to treating non-Muslims equally and being willing to make peace with India.[31]

Surprisingly, the training and ethos of most of the British 'seminaries' indicates only minor concessions have been made to their new location in Britain. The syllabus is often a thinned-down version of what is taught in South Asia. In the case of the Deobandi 'school of thought', the focus is on mastering Arabic to understand the Qur'an and canonical collections of 'Hadith'. There is minimal study of Qur'anic commentaries and Islamic law, no Islamic history beyond the first couple of generations after Muhammad's death, and no Islamic philosophy. The medium of instruction often remains Urdu. Furthermore, even if students study the few A-levels taught in such institutions – Arabic, Urdu, ICT, law and accountancy – their knowledge of British society, its history, culture and institutions, will remain minimal. One other worrying import into Britain has been an increase of intra-Muslim sectarian bigotry with the creation of Saudi supported Salafi mosques, which often embody a literalist understanding of texts and are intolerant of other Islamic groups, such as Shi'i and Sufi.[32] Such bigotry was evident in the *Dispatches* programme broadcast on the 14 February 2011: 'Lessons in Hatred and Violence'.[33]

Peering into the future

It is clear that a new generation of young British Muslim leaders and celebrities is emerging. In the media, one observes the likes of the feisty Saira Khan of *The Apprentice* fame. In sport, one sees the boxer Amir Khan and the cricketer Sajid Mahmood. In the social sciences, younger academics are emerging. In the last election there were a number of Muslim MPs returned, three of whom were women. There are some 20-plus Muslim peers in the House of Lords, male and female. One of the latter, the redoubtable Baroness Sayeeda Warsi, is the first Muslim woman in cabinet. Locally, there are well over 200 councillors including a few lord mayors, past and present.

The previous government invested in imam training, developing women's and young people's networks.[34] In all, British Muslims have generated a huge amount of creativity: there are websites for progressive Muslims, secular Muslims, even ex-Muslims, as well as an explosion of traditional Sunni sites. It is clear that what counts as Muslim identity will continue to be constructed, contested and agonized over in the foreseeable future. The Cambridge University project – 'Contextualising Islam in Britain: Exploratory Perspectives' (2009) – with its refreshing self-criticism, bodes well for the future.[35]

However, so long as the war on terror continues, and conflicts in Afghanistan and Pakistan drag on, relations with sections of the Muslim communities will remain fraught, especially for those who share the same ethnicity and sectarian identity as the Taliban.[36] In the long term, the most important work often goes on unnoticed, such as British institutions opening their doors to Muslims and being willing to negotiate reasonable accommodations to Muslim-specific needs, whether housing associations, the Scouts or churches.[37] The proliferation of local and national initiatives touched on in this work involving Christians and Muslims, whether scriptural reasoning, innovative projects involving Muslims in local churches and cathedrals, or the national Christian Muslim Forum, will become ever more important as communities have to negotiate the impact of deepening recession and the shift to the right across Europe.[38]

Notes

1 www.isb.org.uk.

2 See Philip Jenkins, *God's Continent: Christianity, Islam, and Europe's Religious Crisis* (Oxford: Oxford University Press, 2007). The best short work exploring key theological, political and ethical issues in Christian–Muslim encounter is Christian W. Troll's *Dialogue & Difference: Clarity in Christian–Muslim Relations* (New York: Orbis, 2009). It is the fruit of 40 years of study and engagement by a leading Jesuit scholar.

3 For an interesting insight into 'British Arab Perspectives on religion, politics and "the public"' – especially in contrast to British Pakistani attitudes – see chapter 6 in Peter Hopkins and Richard Gale (eds), *Muslims in Britain: Race, Place and Identities* (Edinburgh: Edinburgh University Press, 2009).

4 See R. Pauly, *Islam in Europe: Integration or Marginalization?* (Aldershot: Ashgate, 2004).

5 Sughra Ahmed, *Seen and Not Heard: Voices of Young British Muslims*, Policy Research Centre, Islamic Foundation, 2009, pp. 39–40.

6 *British Muslims and Education* (Open Society Institute, 2005).

7 See H. Ansari, *The Infidel Within: Muslims in Britain since 1800* (London: Hurst & Co., 2004), pp. 191, 200.

8 Listed in S. R. Ameli's *Globalization, Americanization and British Muslim Identity* (London: Islamic College for Advanced Studies Press, 2002).

9 The picture is not all rosy, however. See G. Singh, 'A city of surprises: urban multiculturalism and the "Leicester model"' in N. Ali et al. (eds), *A Postcolonial People: South Asians in Britain* (London: Hurst & Co., 2006) pp. 291–304.

10 For many such developments see my *Young, British and Muslim* (London: Continuum, 2007).

11 The term 'Islamist' is a shorthand for an ideological reading of Islam which emerges in the 1920s and 1930s in Egypt and India. It is developed by the products of modernity – journalists and teachers – rather than the 'ulama – the generic term for Islam's religious specialists who are trained in traditional centres of Islamic study. The Islamists were impatient of the institutional world of the 'ulama which they considered had fossilized and was unable to address the intellectual challenges facing Muslim elites exposed to new Western ideologies of nationalism, fascism and communism. They reconfigure Islam as a superior political ideology to such imports. See Roxanne L. Euben and Muhammad Qasim Zaman (eds), *Princeton Readings in Islamist Thought: Texts and Contexts from al-Banna to Bin Laden* (New Jersey: Princeton University Press, 2009). For Hizb ut-Tahrir, see *Young, British and Muslim*.

12 By the autumn of 2010 'Muslims' in prison had passed 10,000 or 12.8 per cent of the prison population, which is a truly worrying statistic. This figure was shared at a conference at the Markfield Centre in Leicester, on 9 October 2010, in a talk given by the Muslim adviser on prisons to the Home Office.

13 For the latter, see Unni Wikan, *Generous Betrayal: Politics of Culture in the New Europe* (Chicago: University of Chicago Press, 2002), and Marie Macey, *Multiculturalism, Religion and Women: Doing Harm by Doing Good?* (London: Palgrave Macmillan, 2009).

14 Tariq Modood, *Multicultural Politics: Racism, Ethnicity and Muslims in Britain* (Edinburgh: Edinburgh University Press, 2005), p. 160.

15 See Y. Samad, 'Media and Muslim identity: intersections of generation and gender', *Innovation*, 11:4 (1998), pp. 425–38.

16 See Maleiha Malik (ed.), *Anti-Muslim Prejudice, Past and Present* (London: Routledge, 2010), and Andrew Shrylock (ed.), *Islamophobia/Islamophilia: Beyond the Politics of Enemy and Friend* (Bloomington: Indiana University Press, 2010).

17 See Ahmed, *Seen and Not Heard*, pp. 42–3.

18 Ibid., p. 64.

19 See *Young, British and Muslim*, pp. 46–53.

20 The quotations are taken from Saeed Khan's paper, 'The phenomenon of dual nihilism among British Muslim youth', delivered at the Association of Muslim Social Scientists' Conference – 'Muslim Youth: Challenges, Opportunities and Expectations' – at the University of Chester, 20–22 March, 2009. I am grateful to Saeed for sending me a copy of his paper.

21 S. M. Atif Imtiaz, *Wandering Lonely in a Crowd: Reflections on the Muslim Condition in the West* (Markfield: Kube Publishing, 2011), pp. xi, 85, 87.

22 Z. Badawi, *Islam in Britain* (London: Ta Ha Publications, 1981), p. 27. This is beginning to change with the establishment in 1997 of the European Council for Fatwa and Research in Dublin – see Alexandre Caeiro, 'Transnational ulama, European fatwas, and Islamic authority: a case study of the European Council for Fatwa and Research' in Martin van Bruinessen and Stefano Allievi (eds), *Producing Islamic Knowledge: Transmission and Dissemination in Western Europe* (London: Routledge, 2011).

23 S. Z. Abedin, 'Minority Crises, Majority Options', in T. Hashmi and H. Mutalib (eds), *Islam, Muslims and the Modern State* (London: Palgrave Macmillan, 1994), p. 36.

24 A. Siddiqui, *Christian–Muslim Dialogue in the Twentieth Century* (London: Macmillan, 1997), p. 196.

25 A. Siddiqui, 'Fifty Years of Christian–Muslim Relations: Exploring and Engaging in a New Relationship', *IslamoChristiana*, 26, 2000, 51–77 (73). There are a few exceptions to this. The Muslim College – the creation of the late Sheikh Dr Zaki Badawi – runs courses for Muslim scholars addressed by clergy and rabbis. The Markfield Institute in Leicester runs modules on chaplaincy involving local clergy. And a promising new initiative has just begun at Cambridge – www.cambridgemuslimcollege.org – whereby a course

is being developed to address such lacunae. On its website a number of CMC Papers can be downloaded. No. 1 is entitled 'Some Reflections on Principles of Islamic Education within a Western Context', and itemizes the enormity of the challenges ahead.

26 *Wandering Lonely in a Crowd*, p. 57.

27 E. Moosa, 'Introduction' to F. Rahman, *Revival and Reform in Islam* (Oxford: Oneworld, 2000), p. 26.

28 www.mulimsinbritain.org.

29 See Jonathan Birt and Philip Lewis, 'The Pattern of Islamic Reform in Britain: The Deobandis between intra-Muslim Sectarianism and Engagement with Wider Society', in Bruinessen and Allievi, *Producing Islamic Knowledge*, pp. 91–120.

30 See Ron Geaves, 'Drawing on the past to transform the present: contemporary challenges for training and preparing British imams', *Journal of Muslim Minority Affairs*, 28/1, (2008), 99–112.

31 See Tariq Rahman, 'Madrasas: The Potential for Violence in Pakistan?', in J. Malik (ed.), *Madrasas in South Asia: Teaching Terror?* (Abingdon: Routledge, 2008), pp. 61–84.

32 For Britain, see Sadek Hamid's 'The Attraction of "Authentic Islam": Salafism and British Muslim Youth', in Roger Meijer (ed.), *Global Salafism: Islam's New Religious Movement* (London: Hurst, 2009).

33 The private Muslim school in Birmingham that featured in the programme as pumping out anti-Muslim sectarian bile, as well as hatred of Western society and other faiths, such as Hinduism and Judaism, belonged to the Deobandi 'school of thought'. For more on the internal debates within this tradition, see chapter 4 of *Young, British and Muslim*. For a sombre comment on such 'seminaries', see The Woolf Institute of Abrahamic Faiths, 'The Training of Religious Leaders in the UK: A Survey of Jewish, Christian & Muslim Seminaries' (Cambridge: n.p., 2008). Citation from executive summary. The report can be downloaded from www.woolfinstitute.cam.ac.uk.

34 See Birt and Lewis.

35 This report – which can be downloaded – is the first, to my knowledge, that has engaged all Muslim schools of thought, Muslim academics and activists. Moreover, it pulls no punches in identifying some of the intellectual challenges facing the Islamic tradition in Britain, whether the need to reconnect Islamic law and ethics, why Muslims can and should affirm 'procedural secularism', a critique of utopian readings of politics undergirding much of 'Islamism', to the need to move from a traditional discourse of submission and subject to one of citizen and responsibility.

36 See Ayesha Jalal, *Partisans of Allah: Jihad in South Asia* (Cambridge, MA: Harvard University Press, 2008)

37 See Richard Phillips (ed.), *Muslim Spaces of Hope* (London: Zed Books, 2009). For one city-wide example of Christian involvement, see P. Lewis, 'For the Peace of the City: Bradford – A Case Study in Developing Inter-Community and Inter-Religious Relations', in Stephen R. Goodwin, *World Christianity in Muslim Encounters: Essays in Memory of David A. Kerr,* vol. 2 (London: Continuum, 2009), pp. 273–86. For a good overview of patterns of

principled accommodation and cooperation between churches and mosques, Christians and Muslims, see the website for the Christian Muslim Forum: www.christianmuslimfrum.org.

38 For a disturbing picture of the increased salience of the BNP in Britain and how it foments and capitalizes on fear of Islam, especially where there are large Pakistani communities, see Robert Ford and Mathew J. Goodwin, 'Angry white men: individual and contextual predictors of support for the British National Party', *Political Studies* 58 (2010), 1–25.

4

Islamophobia

Nuzhat Ali

Against the background of our recent history, where deepening fear and suspicion following 11 September 2001 and 7 July 2005 make the role of a faithful, politically engaged Muslim citizen in Britain harder and harder, Nuzhat Ali meditates upon the Qur'anic insight that difference is the root, not of division, but of recognition and deepening acquaintance. She traces a difficult journey from September 2001 to the present, one where personal and global events map in poignant contrast against each other. She looks at her role as mediator, and the ways in which this role makes her a locus of the conflict and division she attempts to bridge. And she looks to the importance of friendship in the slow, fragile process of building trust and shared responsibility between the different communities of Bradford.

O mankind! We created you from a single (pair) of a male and a female, and made you into nations and tribes, that ye may know each other not that ye may despise (each other). Verily the most honoured of you in the sight of God is (he who is) the most righteous of you. And God has full knowledge and is well acquainted with all things. (Qur'an Chapter 49, verse 13)

My wedding anniversary is 11th September. On that fateful day in 2001, with Maroof my husband, I was part of a team delivering a conference we had helped to organize. Bradford Council had produced a document entitled Bradford Vision 2020, setting out a vision for that city for the year 2020. We decided that, as it was predicted that Muslims would be the largest minority community, it would be a good idea to bring an Islamic perspective to the process. The event was attended by people from across the city, and it was a great success. During the middle of the afternoon one of the attendees stood up to make an announcement. He had just received a text message to say the Twin Towers had been 'bombed' and that he hoped 'our Muslim friends are not implicated in this'.

As we drove home there was an ominous stillness: no children playing on the street, an atmosphere of heaviness had descended, a subconscious realization that the world had changed forever. I remember feeling sick with fear and worry, praying fervently that Muslims were not involved in the attacks. We were not to know the full extent of the disaster until we watched the dreadful images on the TV. We cancelled our anniversary dinner and spent an evening in subdued shock. That night the fears in my subconscious translated into a nightmare: faceless men broke into my home, took my husband and myself and our children away.

For many people this scenario has become a reality: detention without charge, imprisonment without trial in Belmarsh, and house arrests. A young man, a British citizen, at home one evening in Islamabad was playing solitaire to unwind. A knock on the door led to arrest and three years in Guantanamo Bay before he was released without charge. That young man, Moazzem Beg, is now involved in attempts to highlight the plight of innocent people and obtain their freedom. Closer to home, dawn in Bradford and a family is awoken by aggressive knocking on the door. The house is searched, computers and laptops confiscated, the father, a close friend of ours, is arrested. He recalls his mother-in-law asking the policemen if they would like a cup of tea (how British can you get?) before he is taken away. His life came to a standstill for six months before he was cleared of any wrongdoing. He has been waiting for over a year now to get security clearance to start a new job, even though no charges were ever bought against him.

For months after 9/11 we felt that, as Muslims, we had to justify ourselves constantly; to apologize for a crime to which none of us had been party, and which the vast majority of us did not condone. My world changed that 11 September. I felt stripped of an innocence and optimism about life. I look at my children growing up now and wonder if they will be allowed to prove themselves like anyone else, or if they will only ever be seen as Muslims, as one of 'them'. How will it affect their life chances? Where will they belong?

Despite the initial feeling of sorrow, empathy and solidarity post-9/11, the words of George W. Bush – 'you are either with us or against us' – turned those feelings into a combination of fear and anger. I remember the helplessness and powerlessness as the world watched the beginning of an illegal war which contravened international law, and in the face of huge public opposition. A conviction started to form that the Muslim community were the new Jews of Europe.

There was also a new fear that was vocalized in whispers and subdued voices. Maybe, we hoped, if we didn't say it aloud then hopefully – please God – it would not ever happen. But it did. And it happened again on a day of personal celebration.

It was 6 July 2005. I had finished a three-year degree in Education that summer and it was the date I received my results. I had been awarded a first class honours degree. I was overjoyed. It had been difficult with a young family to care for, but I had thoroughly enjoyed it. But my happiness was short lived. I had awoken on 7 July with a warm glow which faded very quickly when my husband rang me from work to tell me a terrorist attack had taken place in London. The act we had dreaded the most had happened. How would this affect us? I had already felt intimidated about being in certain places where the majority of people were not Muslims. I remember a middle-aged drunk telling me I should go back to Karachi. Some youths in a car pointed a finger gun at my husband's head, mouthing 'boom'.

I had become involved in community work in the early 1990s. During that time I defined my role as trying to help provide a greater understanding of Islam, to the second and third generations of Muslims as well as the wider society of which we were a part.

There needed to be a sense of belonging, of greater responsibility to each other, of an acceptance with respect. However, in the last eight years I have felt as if I'm straddling two boats, trying to bridge the growing divide between two communities, to convince both of the positive attributes of the other. Sometimes the water of life under my feet reflects a calm phase, but most of the time these days the waters are stormy, angry. It seems that there has to be someone responsible for everything that's going wrong, and Muslims have been identified as the weakest link. You feel scapegoated when there are those who would have all symbols of Islam removed from view.

It is very difficult to be a Muslim and not be affected by politics. Too often I experience a sense of frustration as I watch and listen to so-called 'experts' on Islam, shaping views and opinions as millions of people watch. I feel afraid of how attitudes may turn into actions, either in defence of identity, or aggressively, from those who fear an attack on their values and way of life.

It is very easy, in today's atmosphere, for organizations such as the British National Party or the English Defence League to take advantage of the real concerns of ordinary people. The tolerant British people are fast becoming a very intolerant nation when it comes to Muslims. Because of the actions of a few, it seems that all those who profess the Islamic faith are legitimate targets. Politicians who do not understand, or choose to portray Muslims in a negative light, leave Muslims frustrated at the misrepresentation. And then, Muslims see the West, particularly America, assuming the role of moral policeman of the world, but failing miserably to win over hearts and minds. And so we have two camps, each claiming victimhood.

As I write, the English Defence League want to march in Bradford in August (2010), to exercise the right to freedom of speech and association regardless of the consequences. Because there are consequences. As a Muslim I take seriously my responsibility and accountability before Allah, God. I also distinguish between religion and politics, socio-economics and nationalism: so many of these issues are political, not religious at all. Muslims themselves have, often unwittingly, given the opportunity for those who oppose them to turn political and cultural issues into religious ones. The lack of a core, central leadership, or an icon such as Nelson Mandela, Mahatma Ghandi, Martin Luther King or Malcolm X, has meant a lack of a voice of reason and reflection to speak on our behalf. There are as many 'leaders' within Islam as there are points of view. So when it comes to articulating a balanced, moderate vision of the *Umatun wasatan* (the balanced community) described in the Holy Qur'an, this 'version' of Islam can be questioned with 'Aah, but ... YOU are saying this, but the majority of your community don't feel this way do they?' In those circumstances, what does one say? 'Yes, that's true – but I'm the one that is right!' It does not help that anyone and everyone from Anjem Choudary to Nick Griffin are the new experts on Islam. Both have misrepresented Islam in their own way.

I cringe every time Choudary makes an appearance on the television, usually on a prime time spot. So many times over the last few years I have heard the words 'Why are the "moderate" Muslim voices not heard?' It is not because the voices are not there, but because they are not sensationalist enough for the media spin. I am not in control; I am powerless when it comes to having my voice heard. I can shout as loud as I like, but if there is no one listening then what does it matter?

There needs to be recognition of the difference between constructive criticism and debate and those who go out of their way to cause offence. If I shout 'Islamophobia' because I find something offensive, it's not because I want to shut down the debate, but because I want recognition of the fact that for people of faith, any faith, there are some things that are sacrosanct and should not be defiled. If I consider that someone is disrespectful to what I regard as sacred, it's not because I am taking the higher moral ground, but because of the concept in Urdu of *ghayrat*. The term does not translate into a single word in English: it encompasses self-respect, dignity and pride, but without a loss of humility. Every human being fears the loss of *ghayrat* because it is grounded in our God-given intellect. Each person wants to be respected and to live in dignity; without it we stop being truly human. Offence was rightly taken at photographs coming out of Abu Ghraib in Iraq.

The EDL march in Bradford was advertised as 'the Big One' and it wasn't long before the intention became clear: to cause disruption and mayhem on the streets of Bradford by inciting the young Muslim men to violence. Many in the city feared a repeat of the 2001 riots. Over the summer, activity in the city was geared towards making sure that Bradford was not tarnished again. The atmosphere in the city became increasingly apprehensive as 28 August approached, and the level of positive concern was extremely encouraging. Strong relationships were there, across divides of difference, which formed a strong resilient backbone to maintain peace in Bradford. Bradford Women for Peace came together to send out a message of peace and solidarity in Bradford city centre on 27 August. Being part of that gathering meant a lot to me, and even though I was nervous (as we all were) about the following day, it gave me hope and confidence that we could pull through.

It was Ramadan, the month of fasting, peace and blessings, of practising patience and self-restraint. It involved long days in the hottest time of the year. If the EDL had wanted a fight, they simply chose the worst time of the year! I was helping out at one of the many events being held during that Saturday. As I was driving down to the venue, the roads were eerily silent. It was as if the whole city was holding its breath, just waiting for the day to be over.

I wonder whether the EDL really do have genuine reasons for their Islamophobia. Without a doubt the landscape of Europe has changed drastically in the last 20 or so years. But is this reason enough to have the kind of hatred that can readily be seen on YouTube videos of the event? Everything is so negative. Where is the positive message of being British? The behaviour of the members on 28 September couldn't have been less British. The local press reported how demonstrators had urinated and defecated where they had stood.

So why do members of the EDL have such views? A close friend and active community member, Wahida Shaffi, spent some time talking to a group of young men who were members of the EDL. She asked them why they were involved with the group; they responded with the fact that they weren't against Muslims in general, but were against terrorists and radicals. They were very polite. She had the impression that this was a conditioned response; that they had come ready for a fight, fired up to protest against 'Muslims causing trouble', resentful that the 'Asian lot get most of the stuff'. Wahida was in close range; she could hear the chants of the men. They were trying to incite the Asian men by using derogatory statements about 'Allah'.

In 2008 I was selected to work as the interfaith development officer at Bradford Cathedral, thanks to the efforts of the then Canon, Frances Ward. I was the second Muslim to work in a cathedral in the UK, and it was a real privilege. It wasn't always easy for Frances to secure the funding and do the groundwork with regard to people's attitudes, but she knew how important it was for people to have their perceptions challenged. We worked together to model a relationship based on real friendship which tried to understand and respect the differences within our faith traditions as well as celebrating the similarities. But more than that, our relationship was based on the fact that we were human beings together; we were friends. Becoming accepted by the congregation at the cathedral was a gradual process: I simply was true to myself, and open to them, and it seemed to work. There is progress when people stop being afraid of what they might lose. For Muslims that is often their Islamic identity, which is held sometimes too conservatively; for others it may be British values.

Muslims need to understand the responsibility they have to reflect the merciful nature of the Creator, especially by emulating the Prophet Muhammad, whom he sent as a mercy to the worlds. They have to be sure that it is not their actions that creates Islamophobia. Many times it is the outward austere and sometimes even frightening appearance that can have a negative effect. It was the attitude of the Prophet towards others, including and sometimes especially those who were not Muslims, that commended him and his faith to others. We, as Muslims, more often than not are not very good at absorbing this. With the best of intentions, we have a habit of thinking individually – me, myself and I: how can I show greater piety? By the length of my beard? The shortness of my *thawb* (long overshirt)? ...or the blackness of my niqab? Do we ever stop to consider what kind of impression we create – of Islam, of Muslims? I started with a verse from the Holy Qur'an

> O mankind! We created you from a single (pair) of a male and a female, and made you into nations and tribes, that ye may know each other not that ye may despise (each other). Verily the most honoured of you in the sight of God is (he who is) the most righteous of you. And God has full knowledge and is well acquainted with all things. (Qur'an Chapter 49, verse 13)

The translation needs clarification. The word *ta'aruf* in the passage is translated 'to know' but actually goes much further than that – *ta'aruf* means to be introduced to someone in order to get to know them. When someone is introduced to us we find out more about them: their likes, dislikes, where they live and work, what their family is like, and so on. This builds up a picture for us of another human being with aspirations, hopes, worries and fears. It makes them 'real' for us, and so it becomes far harder to dehumanize them. My hope is that we will recognize, through our common humanity, the need to create a society, and indeed a world, where acceptance and respect of difference becomes the norm. We have to regain the ability to think critically for ourselves and try to understand issues we are faced with, coming to our own well-informed judgements, rather than being brainwashed by the media, our politicians or our religious leadership. Indeed, religious literacy amongst ordinary people is becoming more and more important if we are to create cohesive and resilient communities. In a world where fear and the fragmentation of society and social, economic and political divides become ever greater, the need to focus on friendship and the common values that unite us becomes increasingly necessary.

5

Much Ado About Nothing at Bradford Cathedral

Frances Ward

Behind Frances Ward's narrative of her engagement with the city of Bradford in becoming the new residentiary canon of its cathedral, lies an ancient understanding of humane citizenship. Although its roots lie in a very masculine Aristotelian philia, in this case it is offered through the gift of women's friendship, brought into being in the gentler privacies of informal conversation, and then modelled in a variety of public contexts as a means to robust and grounded dialogue between faiths which is political in the best sense – of the polis, the shared city of which all are citizens. That women speak in this way is of particular importance, for at the heart of what they discuss is the silencing of women within the polis. Frances Ward writes both of the possibilities and the limits of public friendship between women of different faiths in an atmosphere of fear; of compromise; of integrity. She leaves us with a profound question, simultaneously private and public: where does true courtesy lie?

I first met Wahida Shaffi one day in October 2006. I had shortly returned from ten days in Pakistan – part of an induction into my new role as residentiary canon at Bradford Cathedral. We met outside St Paul's Church in Manningham, in Bradford, and we walked to the local Lister Park, which was one of her favourite places. Wahida had been born and grew up in the area; as we sat on a bench overlooking the central boating lake, one of her brothers walked by. We spoke at length.

I talked of those ten days in Pakistan, and was unsure how open I could be. I certainly didn't want to cause offence, given that Pakistan was her parents' homeland. I had been shocked by the lack of women in public space and the intense activity we'd witnessed – as we met with leading political commentators, the legal profession, human rights activists and government officials – to repeal the 'hudud ordinances' and the blasphemy laws. Wahida wasn't at all defensive and so I continued to talk.

She heard me say that I had come back profoundly grateful for the things I take for granted in Britain: that she and I could sit here, on a park bench, and talk; the health service, good quality state education. For we had visited a rural madrassah near Mensehra, where only boys received an education – based upon learning the Qur'an, of course. English was taught in this more enlightened madrassah, but it was antediluvian, judging by the textbooks. I told her that the headteacher of the madrassah had been accompanied by a little girl of 6 or so, in a red dress. She was obviously bright as she tried to follow the conversation, and I'd asked him if she would be educated, and he had said no. And I'd been left thinking of her often since then, and wondering about her life and what it would hold, one of the 40 plus per cent of women who are illiterate in the population.

Wahida told me about her parents: how her father had crossed at partition in 1947, a boy of 10, terrified as he hid in ditches. How they had come, when the reservoir was built at Mirpur, to Bradford, in response to the need for workers in the textile industry. How neither of her parents could read or write; how proud they had been, when she received a First in her MA in International Relations from the Peace Studies Department, and Jim Whitman, her supervisor, had come to the ceremony and knelt at her mother's feet to say how proud they should be of her.

She had trained as a social worker, and after a time in youth work, now worked freelance as a community facilitator. Her latest project was with the Joseph Rowntree Foundation, a project which has been designed to give women skills to use digital media to tell their own stories. The project *Women Working Towards Excellence: Our Stories, Our Lives* was about empowering women within the communities around them. Wahida knew many who were isolated, in families with real intra-generational difficulties. I spoke about how important it was that women were more involved in interfaith work, how often it seemed that it was a male, talking-heads business, with few resilient relationships of trust. I spoke about how women needed to make a crucial transition from the private world of home and local community and face the public square, finding strategic ways of ensuring that their voices were heard.

That was 2006. Since then, after four years, my whole worldview has changed. Previously, I'd been a vicar in Bury, Lancashire, and that is what sparked my interest in Islam: I had been chair of governors at a primary school which had a high intake of Muslim-heritage children. I had wanted to know more about what it meant for Britain, locally and nationally, that Muslim-heritage people now had significant and increasing populations in most major cities and towns. Interfaith engagement seemed high on the agenda for some in the Church of England,[1] but for others it didn't seem to register at all – until 11 September 2001 and 7 July 2005, of course. Where better than Bradford to learn more?

The cathedral in Bradford had been through some difficult times. A failed Millennium project had left it with no clergy, and less money. We had a new dean, David Ison, and two new residentiary canons. Together we needed to get the cathedral on its feet again, to help an ageing congregation feel loved after they'd been battered by events, and draw in new worshippers. It was important to recover credibility within the city after many had lent money and seen it disappear. We were tasked with building a sense of purpose and engagement, and faced the fundamental question: what was the cathedral there for, anyway?

It is a beautiful building, with an interesting history – certainly the oldest building in a city that has seen its heart ripped out through successive attempts at regeneration. For all of my four years, the cathedral presided over 'The Hole': a Westfield development that ground to a halt as the economic downturn hit in 2008. We have next to no visitors, apart from children on educational visits from schools in the surrounding region. The building is difficult to find and the lack of car parking is a constant deterrent.

So what was the purpose of the cathedral in a city that, for many Yorkshire folk, had seen better days? There are those who remember it as a thriving shopping centre that, in earlier times, surpassed Harrogate, or Ilkley, or even Leeds; they remember it as a city rich on the pickings of the wool trade, which flourished on a shrewd business sense and canny connections around the world. In pockets one will still find this: an entrepreneurial spirit that has developed to meet markets in unexpected ways, and a business sense that takes advantage of the low costs of labour and property. I have met the man who has the world monopoly in manufacturing the wires needed for electric blankets, supplying China. I have met a wool man who still trades in the finest worsted to the Far East, and around the world; importing wool from Geelong in Australia, which is processed in Italy, and sold through Bradford. If you wander around the city centre, though, such resilient wealth is not apparent. Retail is desperate, though an imaginative Waterstones within the old Wool Exchange hints at what might be done. Many people with resources do not live in city-centre Bradford anymore; they certainly don't shop there. Nightlife happens in Leeds.

The next census is due in 2011, and so population statistics available before then are inevitably out of date and unreliable in this city that changes fast. All the predictions are that Bradford is increasingly populated by Asian-heritage citizens, and that the population is increasingly younger. The city has seen its share of unrest – disturbances in 1995 and in 2001 – and it lives with the threat that the city centre will be targeted by extremist groups who might pounce as soon as any trigger goes off, shipping people in to stir trouble. An attempt at this was made in August 2010, but came to very little, mainly because concerned civic leaders, the council and the police worked well to develop strategies to dispel any threat.

It is an edgy city, but there are some tremendous people living and working to enhance the common good. The Joseph Rowntree Foundation has made a long-term commitment to research poverty in and around Bradford; the Programme for a Peaceful City, based at the university, continues to reflect and act to build civic resilience. The council often fails to exert a strong leadership, and one comes across a deep suspicion of 'religion', especially from people who are not particularly religiously literate, to use Lord Parekh's expression. For them, religion of all forms is 'a chaos monster', as Luke Bretherton has characterized it, to be avoided at all costs. How could the cathedral represent itself as a rational power for the common good to councillors who, if they had heard of the place, remembered it only as 'the failed Millennium project'? How might the cathedral make friends within the Muslim-heritage communities, especially when there was no significant history of such outreach amongst clergy predecessors?

There were some doors to push open. A Faiths Forum is funded by the council, and there are some connections with the Council of Mosques, but nothing ongoing and structural. Very significantly, Philip Lewis lived and worked in the city, and he is an expert in Christian–Muslim relations with an international reputation. But as I arrived, I wondered where the women were, and how actively they were engaged in developing interfaith relations. It didn't take long to find them, though it did take slightly longer to build trusting friendships. There were a number of lively and interesting women, but only one or two were present on the Faiths Forum, and their voices were rarely heard on the Council of Mosques.

It was one of those memorable conversations, with Wahida, that day in Lister Park. A week or so later, we went to Keighley, to an interfaith evening, and as we travelled in the car on the way home, she described to me some other Christian friends of hers who spoke of their desire that she would become a Christian. How to respond? I said that I would find it difficult if I thought that our friendship had that as an agenda – hidden or otherwise. I said that both our religions take conversion seriously, but that I felt I commended Christ best through respecting her faith as a Muslim, and learning what I could from her about her religion. She told me how, as she grew up, there was a Christian woman as a neighbour, who was very kind to her. It was an important moment in our growing friendship, and over the months ahead we continued to think about friendship – not just as something private, but how it could be a public good as well.

Then in the summer of 2007, the cathedral hosted a performance of Shakespeare's *Much Ado about Nothing*. The producer, Damien O'Keeffe, told me about the play, and how the main female character feigns death as she is dishonoured at the altar. I went home and read it. My hunch was right; this would be really interesting to discuss within a group of women. The issues were all there: Shakespeare was exploring the role of women and their self-determination with regard to significant partnerships within a culture of patriarchy and honour. So I talked with Wahida about the idea, and asked her to suggest two other Muslim women. I invited another Christian minister and a friend of mine who was atheist and had recently entered a civil partnership. With some funding from the Christian Muslim Forum we were able to tape our conversations to a professional standard, and so the six of us met before the play was performed to begin the conversation. Each of us talked about our lives with a frankness and openness that was moving. We then watched the play together, and met again a few days later. Here is Wahida in a short extract, illustrating how the play enabled issues to be discussed which often are considered too sensitive to be addressed. She picks up on the theme of war and threat that seems to hang over the play:

> But going back to what you were talking about in terms of this darker figure clouding over any light that seems to be appearing, it's really interesting as a parallel to some of the things we see in Britain but also elsewhere around honour killings as well. The recent example I think was of a young woman. I think she was pregnant as well and she was stabbed to death – it made the national media – and again, like, this false sense of what it means to kill another human being: there's no

justification for that. And I think the worst thing that people can do, and generally do, is to make these gross accusations. As is the case with Leonato and Claudio and Don Pedro who make a gross accusation that casts aspersions on Hero's reputation, her honour. Similarly gross accusations are made and people take that one step – in the case of Hero it was a mock death; but in the case of reality, Pakistan has one of the highest rates of honour killings in the world and that's a fact and at the same time we're seeing similar things in other places and I think it's wrong. The fact that people can accuse people but at the same time take that one step further in terms of murder is something that is just terrible.

Very quickly the play enabled the six women to engage with what mattered against the backdrop of the communities of Bradford where we all lived. And one of the most interesting discussions was about honour. The play, written in the last few years of the sixteenth century, explores the way in which male honour needs to be upheld when it is challenged. The bride-to-be, Hero, is accused falsely of infidelity before her marriage to Claudio. He confronts her at the wedding ceremony; she swoons, and the friar, who is officiating at the service, declares her dead. She isn't really, and returns to life when all have realized the mistake; marries Claudio, and all are reconciled. Nuzhat, here, picked up on the theme:

I don't think they consider it as murder, though. It's an act of war – you know, coming back to the differences between love and war, but again it comes down to whose honour? What about Hero? What about her dignity? What about her honour – or her feelings? And that's never actually discussed. It's always the father's feelings, or Claudio's feelings. They're the ones who have been trampled on. They're the ones whose honour has been trampled on. Nowhere is it discussed; actually it's not them who are being accused. It's Hero who's being accused and no body's actually saying, well, how do you feel about this? But a lot of the stuff around honour killings, again, it's a question of whose honour? Yeah. And is the person actually doing anything wrong? Who's making those rules? And if you look, it will be a patriarch in a family somewhere who's deciding. Right now, in Bradford, I could tell you that there is a matriarch or a patriarch like this – yeah, because although we're focusing on men, women can inflict this on other women as well. Sometimes when you have a very strong matriarch the men in the family actually become quite weak and don't stand up to her because they say, 'Well, you know, this is my mum, I have to honour her, I have to respect her.' They may not show that same honour or respect towards their wife and her opinion, or to their daughter and her opinion, but that mother figure will become someone who's infallible in many respects and that also can have that very detrimental effect. Whose honour is it? If you are upholding the family honour – what family, or caste or tribe?

Using a play by Shakespeare enabled all of us to sidestep either set of scriptures – the Bible, the Qur'an – into ground where we could start to map our concerns about religion, identity, sex, misunderstandings, fallings-out and friendships, some of the issues that can be extremely difficult to talk about. We managed to find a way to go deeper into matters that really concerned us, beyond the superficialities that mark so much of what gets called 'interfaith dialogue'.

Here we began a conversation about what values, or virtues, should inform society at large. This was a beginning: together the women grew closer as they spoke honestly about how each of us was shaped by the significant relationships we had, and how those relationships were negotiated differently in our different cultures and communities. By turning to a text of enduring (and constantly re-emerging) power, the women were able to discuss with a profundity not often reached about such sensitive matters.

How can we foster places and situations where such discussions can happen on a much wider scale? Usually, questions such as these – about honour, for example – are left well alone by social commentators (except for a few brave souls) in Britain today, for fear of causing offence and stirring a sense of identity that is exactly concerned about defending its own honour. Such a stirred 'identity' often has no facility to make room for self-criticism or examination, let alone a sense of forgiveness for those who do wrong. As a nation we need to ask ourselves whether there is a difference, as I think there is, between an ideology of honour and rights that require defence, and the Christian understanding of self-sacrifice and forgiveness. But we are a long way from engaging honestly and respectfully about such a profound difference in moral framework.

At a basic level what Nuzhat, Wahida and I achieved was a friendship that was resilient and non-defensive enough to model publicly the permission needed to break through the constraints of fear that operate so effectively in British society today. We made a start. The following passage was important from the beginning, from Hannah Arendt. She was awarded the Lessing Prize of the Free City of Hamburg in 1959, and her acceptance speech was published as 'On Humanity in Dark Times'. In it she said this:

We are wont to see friendship solely as a phenomenon of intimacy, in which the friends open their hearts to each other unmolested by the world and its demands. Rousseau, not Lessing, is the best advocate of this view, which conforms so well to the basic attitude of the modern individual, who in his alienation from the world can reveal himself only in privacy and in the intimacy of face-to-face encounters. Thus it is hard for us to understand the political relevance of friendship. When, for example, we read in Aristotle that *philia* friendship among citizens is one of the fundamental requirements for the well-being of the City, we tend to think that he was speaking of no more than the absence of factions and civil war within it. But for the Greeks the essence of friendship consisted in discourse. They held that only the constant interchange of talk united citizens in a *polis*. In discourse the political importance of friendship, and the humanness peculiar to it, were made manifest. This converse (in contrast to the intimate talk in which individuals speak about themselves), permeated though it may be by pleasure in the friend's presence, is concerned with the common world, which remains 'inhuman' in a very literal sense unless it is constantly talked about by human beings. For the world is not humane just because it is made by human beings, and it does not become humane just because the human voice sounds in it, but only when it has become the object of discourse. However we are affected by the things of the world, however deeply they may stir and stimulate us, they become human for us only when we can discuss them with our fellows … We humanize what is going on in the world and in ourselves only by speaking of it, and in the course of speaking of it we learn to be human.[2]

What is so important about this passage is how Arendt emphasizes the importance of public discourse rather than the private intimacy of friendship. Of course, friends need to work in private, too, especially if they are consciously building a public friendship. My friendships with women in Bradford were a deliberate attempt to model something different. We have talked, in private, about what might go wrong; we have tried to anticipate what we might disagree about so fundamentally that the friendship would not survive. We have talked about Islamophobia and fear; I have heard from them the very real fears that Muslim-heritage people live with. We have also met white people who have expressed other sorts of fears: fears that Muslims just want to take over; the fear of causing offence if they say the wrong thing. I have heard from Muslims who fear to return to Pakistan to meet a frosty reception because they have colluded with the West; of people who have been kidnapped by the Taliban, with a high ransom – millions of pounds – demanded. There is a lot of fear, and anger, around. Such fears need to be aired in private before they can be tackled in public.

During the summer of 2010 we held three open evenings; the first was on Jesus and Mohammad; the second was on 'Is religion bad for you?'; the third was on 'What does it mean to be British?'. They drew audiences of 30–70. Together Nuzhat and I modelled friendship, extending it so that people present could feel safe enough to explore things that concerned them. It was possible to talk about entryism, victim mentality, education and young people, and all sorts of things. It worked: a public friendship worked because we had done our private homework. With Aristotle's thinking in the background, our friendship began to create a different sort of culture; it was one that enabled a deeper level of engagement about issues that concern us, but which people are often reticent to broach.

Where does such discussion and debate happen? How often do we sit and talk – publicly, rather than privately – to debate and discuss what the common good might look like? Yes, we see it in the media and in Parliament – two obvious places. But where does real, trusting, humanizing conversation happen? Partly what we tried to do at the cathedral was to provide a venue for such conversations to happen in the public sphere: modelling a trusting friendship that enables us to explore stuff that is difficult, even disagreeing in public.

A sense of irony and forgiveness is central. Irony enables one to view oneself with humour and insight, to tease and be teased. Forgiveness is important, too, because inevitably things will be said which should have been left unsaid, or things left undone which should have been done. Without forgiveness, offence is caused; without irony, there is a lack of lightness of touch which is so important as a friendship develops. Cultural texts can open the door, particularly when they establish a distance between the drama of the play and the drama of life: *Much Ado About Nothing* was a case in point. The play enabled those from a variety of backgrounds to reflect with real moral and emotional knowledge on life in Britain today.

But it need not be simply the heritage of English literature that we turn to. Here is Irna's reaction, having seen the play:

Well, you know, it was just like a Bollywood film. It really was. And you know it wasn't so much that yes, it was really serious, but it was so melodramatic: the highs and the lows! I just kept thinking this is just like a bolly, and you know at the end, and yes, I know there's a serious point, but at the end when poor little Hero came back to life, I've seen that scene in a film and it just reminded me of a Bollywood film. And like as I say, it was the plot, the highs and lows, the distance that the characters had travelled, the learning the morals, as well as the harder hitting stuff like the dad, the guilt and all of that.

Cultural forms, and particularly those that deepen moral and emotional knowledge, are a rich resource. Those resources become available when people meet in an atmosphere of openness and enquiry, seeking to explore with each other as friends the treasures of each other's culture and religion. In any good and long-lasting friendship you bring who you are to the other, and you are open and eager to learn more about the person before you. The more understanding you have of your own cultural roots, the richer that engagement will be.

What was exciting about friendship here was taking something that women are often very good at, in private, and sharing it in the public realm. Of course, men do it too: think of David Sheppard and Derek Warlock – the two Bishops of Liverpool whose friendship did much to build links between the Catholic and Protestant communities of that city. But between Christian and Muslim communities, perhaps women have much to offer, being less hidebound by (male) codes of honour, and more able to draw on cultural forms and resources than a patriarchal reliance upon religious text as authoritative.

Even with Wahida and Nuzhat it has been difficult at times. Constantly I feel on my guard lest I stir them into defensiveness. It is fine, so long as I observe the common ground we share, namely, virtue ethics, and the important role that religion can play in public life. But if I start to question the received wisdom about the Prophet Mohammad, for example on whether he really was as open and accepting of women as often presented; or whether there is a contrast between an ethic of honour and forgiveness, and what that might mean in practice, we don't get very far. The fear is deep, if the defensiveness is anything to go by. It's hard to be friends when questions of security – both personal and political – are high on the agenda. It's hard to be a Muslim in Britain today and navigate a way through the different perceptions of Islam without becoming a victim to fear. It's hard to be a friend when you have a victim mentality, or are dominated by resentment and grievance. Neither Nuzhat nor Wahida are victims. But there are areas I know that stir both of them into a forceful defence of their faith and identity. One issue I remember on which Nuzhat and I differed was the Dutch cartoons and the place – the important place, as I would see it – of satire in a healthy society. For Nuzhat, the cartoons were beyond the pale, unacceptable as they caused offence. For me, Christ carried offence and dishonour to the cross, so he is beyond the risk that offence might harm him.

When you come up against such profound differences, it is hard; and for me, the ongoing friendship meant that I never pressed it further than I felt was appropriate. My friendship with each of them, Nuzhat and Wahida, was more important than the issues; or rather, I didn't want to turn it into a conflict between friendship and faith. Perhaps I compromised too much my adherence to Christ, as sometimes I allowed the agenda to be carried by Nuzhat, letting her determine what ground we covered and what we did not. But that seemed right, even if it has left me with frustrations and the desire to proclaim Christ more passionately than I allowed myself. My own fears are there, too. I fear that Christianity is declining and that even if I argued the case for Christ well and cogently, Christ would still be rejected.

Friendship: for its own sake; that real love of someone else; and warmth; and intimacy. I'm someone who loves a good argument, someone who doesn't like slushy relationships that become sentimental and therefore untruthful. But I know that there was a sense in which I was untruthful to myself for the sake of Nuzhat: I agreed with her rather than enter into conflict. Even writing this, I'm aware that I don't want to push the limits too hard: I value her friendship too much. I fear losing her. And I continue to hope that the friendship will deepen so that we will become more truthful about faith, less fearful. I say that I allow her agenda to carry the day: her framing of the questions, her opinions, with my only gentle questioning in response. Or am I being really untrue here? Does my allowing her to dominate betray my own capacity to allow? Where does true courtesy lie?

Having worked in Bradford for those four years, I've found myself reflecting on the role of the Church of England in our national life. Seldom is it patrician in its attitudes any more – the 'Tory party at prayer'. Yes, often it can seem locked away in a very public prison, overly concerned with its own trivial agenda: debates about homosexuality when the world has moved on; an institution seemingly in stalemate over women bishops. But putting such matters to one side, we worked hard in Bradford to find a renewed confidence in its role of creating a culture of hospitality, and thereby contributing to the health of Britain. The potential was there, for a Church of England that could fire up the imagination of the nation, shaping an open, free society that welcomes people of difference and values what they bring. There is a role here, I believe, for a national church that is confident and secure in its own character, with the treasures of its traditions and cultures that can equip us as a corporate nation to face an uncertain future. In many places, the church can take a lead in forming close and resilient friendships with newcomers to Britain, opening its doors, and encouraging other associations and civic organizations to do the same, helping to build a nation where all belong.

Notes
1 The Presence and Engagement Network is a good example. See: http://www. presenceandengagement.org.uk.
2 Hannah Arendt, from 'On Humanity in Dark Times: Thoughts about Lessing', in *Men in Dark Times* (San Diego: Harvest, 1995), pp. 24–5.

6

Via Media

Miriam Mushayi, Imran Manzoor and Javaad Alipoor

From the pun hidden in the group's title, this multifaceted critique does much more than narrate the history of Via Media's inception and development. We also learn the idea from which the group sprang, the context in which it was set up and the ways in which it was modified. We do this both from the inside as part of the process of engagement, and from the outside as the group's funding history pushed it in particular political and administrative directions. But this is also a sharply pertinent reflection on the impoverished nature of political debate and practice in Britain today and the effect this is having on the intelligent young. The group's story also demonstrates, more in sorrow than in anger, the clumsy effects of administrative and political civic agendas driven by fear and misinformation. A wealth of skill and passion in our young is in danger of being wasted, and genuine, analytical, highly informed political engagement is one important remedy for our social ills.

Via Media began as an idea of Imran's. He noticed that the young people who were joining racist groups like the BNP or becoming vulnerable to other kinds of ideological violent extremism had what he described as a contradictory relationship with basic political education. On the one hand they often showed a fundamental lack of knowledge of political structures, or how one effects change in civil society, often lacking even the most basic coordinates with which to understand political history. On the other hand, contrary to certain received opinions, a lot of the young people who have become vulnerable to violent extremism are in fact intelligent, articulate and confident. The question Imran found himself asking was: how could such intelligent young people display such a poor understanding of what constitutes reasoned, critical political thought and action?

Via Media was to develop from this idea into a course. But first we need to put it into context, for it can be seen as the latest in a long series of interventions. Via Media found a home within the PRISM youth project. This had grown out of the Bradford Police Boys Club, an organization set up in the 1930s to deal with the influx of young people from the surrounding countryside into Bradford, where they found nothing to do. Since then it had continued to offer a shooting range downstairs, and a boxing gym on the ground floor. More recently the young people came from the local African Caribbean community, which was by this time dwindling in size, largely because, so it was locally understood, the Leeds and Bradford City Councils had followed a policy of encouraging the members of minority communities to move to areas where they were in a majority. And so African Caribbean people were encouraged to move to the Chapeltown area of Leeds, and people of South Asian origin were encouraged to move to the locality of the PRISM project, where there was already a sizeable population. Such a policy, it was hoped, would change the dynamic of conflict between the young people of South Asian and African Caribbean descent in the area. This can be seen as a classic example of translating a political problem (in this case an obvious issue of crime and policing) into a cultural one (where the main motivating force is seen as the inability of two 'cultures' to interact without harassing each other or causing offence, rendering the issue an object of administrative manoeuvres).

With the appointment of a new director, Bradford Police Boys Club became the Bradford Police Club for Young People. With the intention of bringing in more white people and women, it started off with an alternative curriculum project and grew from there. Over a decade the organization became the PRISM youth project, where now a whole range of programmes is provided, from a city farm for children with learning difficulties, to health projects and an initiative, directed at vulnerable young women from the local community, that does valuable work in building confidence and self-esteem. The project continues to grow, developing work in alternative curricula, and has now advanced to the stage where the organization is looking to be recognized as a school. The organizational capacity and reputation of the PRISM youth project offered Via Media a good home, making this new course possible.

Returning to that question Imran found himself asking – how was it that such intelligent young people could display such a poor understanding of what constitutes reasoned, critical political thought and action? – his response in the first instance was to create a framework that would ground young people in political history, giving them a basic set of coordinates. To begin with, what tended to have the most impact was at the emotional level, particularly the topics in which the young people's understanding was the most stereotyped.

The Palestinian conflict, with its highly-charged impact on many young people, is a good example. Although they would be largely ignorant of the complicated reality of the situation – such as the existence of a large Palestinian Christian community; the historic role of liberal-nationalist and leftist groups in the Palestinian national movement; the early Israeli support for Hamas – the young people were jarred by the brutality of the violence in the conflict. When Via Media helped them to understand the continuing effects of events like the Holocaust, the Deir Yassin massacre and the infamous 'Plan D', a notable difference would emerge in the way the young people presented their views. What was, before, a matter of emotional outrage and anger, became expressed in a calm, measured way. The passion was still there, but now informed by a breadth of knowledge and understanding.

The Via Media course covered a number of topics in the history of Islamic politics and thought as well, providing background to historical solidarities between Jewish and Muslim cultures and peoples and also how Muslims and Jews had come to be perceived as carrying eternal enmities towards each other. Reading history in this way was extended to look at the political development of so-called 'violent extremist' or 'jihadi' interpretations of Islam, from its inception in Nasser's concentration camps to the killing fields of the Algerian civil war, through to the emergence of Ayman al-Zawahari as its alleged 'theoretician' and Bin Laden as its so-called 'Sheikh'. The Muslim young people we worked with came from what could be described rather vaguely as 'traditional' Islamic backgrounds. Contrary to the mass hysteria peddled by the likes of Melanie Phillips, Robert Spencer and so on, places with large Muslim minorities are not 'hub(s) for the promotion, recruitment and financing of ... terror'. In fact, the main problem with teaching this topic to the young people was that they had not heard of anyone other than Bin Laden – a long way from the idea that a large portion of Britain's Muslims constitute some sort of quasi-conspiratorial 'fifth column' of raving al-Qaeda supporters. We covered some Islamic topics, more from a historical than strictly religious perspective, some political topics and ultimately we took the first group to Poland to see the remains of the Auschwitz complex.

As we look back now, with a critical eye, the main change we have made since the first course is to move away from those emotional 'shock tactics' – the way many Holocaust-centred projects teach this issue. We've taken on board the view of some critics that such a pedagogical approach is questionable: young people cannot be shocked or emoted into thinking critically about their society and their place in it.

What we offered soon attracted attention. A number of organiza-tions came and heard about the project and saw what happened. We had funders coming forward offering money for us to make the same provision, although some wanted it on their terms, which were very different from what Imran originally saw as the main drive of the project. Ultimately we were successful, with a very large sum of money donated to us. We began the programme with a new sense of what precisely we were trying to achieve; what worked; what didn't. With funding and a team in place, now with Miriam and Javaad on board, we were able to build up the programme to its present form.

So where did the funding come from? Several streams, from charitable trusts to the state, came forward to say they saw value in the objectives of the work we were delivering. Finally, the funding that we did receive had a very particular agenda: the 'Prevent' agenda. The problems (perceived or otherwise) with this agenda have been discussed at length. In essence, the debate has circled around the following accusations: that it has led to the criminalization of the Muslim community; that group funding that might have been set aside to tackle structural poverty and racism has been redirected into counter-terrorism; that projects felt they were being put over a barrel; that this was the only money available to work with certain communities. Many community organizations felt the pressure to show that they were doing something about violent extremism. The Prevent agenda also fostered the view that violent extremism is the only thing that defines young Muslim men, distinguished by how 'vulnerable' or 'resilient' they are.

The accusation of criminalization is a very interesting one. On the one hand, almost every government strategy document issued on the subject has explicitly denied its reality. On the other, the Institute of Race Relations published a paper on the Prevent agenda in which they constructed a graph of the number of Muslims in a given area against the Prevent funding received – and it showed a direct correlation. Although it is clear that no one in government office thinks that Muslims are inherently liable to turn to terrorism, it is also clear that certain structural patterns have emerged.

The previous government tried to iron out some of these problems with the Contest 2 strategy. But this, too, has not escaped criticism: it has been argued that the focus has enlarged to include not only those who lean towards violence, but also those who have 'extremist' views. There is a worrying ambiguity here, especially in the light of the government's commitment not to criminalize thought or speech. Concretely, we should ask what this means in practice. It seems clear that this new strategy is a reaction to the embarrassment caused by revelations that a lot of the groups that were working in the original Prevent constellation represented what many people saw as the most conservative forms of Islam. This indicates a certain empirical reality within the present day politics of Islam. Those organizations and groups that are most committed to finding a home in a world dominated by Europeans and Americans take a pietistic route. They decide not to get involved in politics and completely renounce armed political causes in any part of the Muslim world, whether explicitly Islamic in character or not. Such groups tend to be those with the most conservative views on gender, sexuality and hermeneutics, and they are also the most sectarian on issues of religious practice.

On the ground, we became aware that the whole strategy (Prevent and Contest 2) was having problems. What had set out to counter extremism ended up alienating communities. If you bought into the Prevent agenda you were viewed with scepticism. Confidence and trust – essential to friendship – that had existed before became eroded.

Conferences and workshops were held to critique the whole agenda. We attended a packed meeting chaired by Liberty and JUST West Yorkshire. A particular sticking point was something called the 'National Indicator 35', against which every local council has to report. Only a few local authorities said that they would not carry out this procedure, which called on them to account for the Preventing Violent Extremism work that was happening in their areas. Bradford was one of them. The National Indicator 35 required teachers, youth workers and others from many public professions to take an active role in monitoring the political development of people in their care. The necessity of friendship and trust – between student and teacher, citizen and politician, or professional and service user – was difficult to sustain when all involved knew that such monitoring was required.

Such political intervention, as it developed, took on a life of its own. Countering it was a real challenge, theoretically and practically. Increasingly, we understood that standard political discourse has developed to strengthen the administrative model of political action, alienating citizens from the principles and ideas that should inspire participation in political processes. Instead, politics is perceived as a series of administrative challenges; the media reducing it to stories about politicians and civil servants making mistakes or poor decisions. This was a long way from a truly participative process where young people could feel involved in making a better world. We saw a correlation between this castrated notion of the political as the space of competing management styles and the growth of extremist politics and groups advocating violence. When serious debates around differences are excluded at the level of political philosophy, disaffected young people are much more likely to be seduced by strong ideology. Via Media has been about opening up a space in which such thought and discussion can take place.

In that space we have found significant success in working with the really 'hard end' referrals. In many such cases, the ability to talk and think deeply with a radical critique blew away the narrow, identity-based ideologies upon which violent extremism is so often based. Interestingly enough, this often put us at odds with other Prevent-funded projects. Where the dominant idea was to encourage young people vulnerable to violent extremism to think less about politics, our answer was always, 'more politics'!

This is done in three ways. First, we develop the faculty of critical thought. This involves actual historical study, as much as it does analytical type skills. We look at controversial historical events with a view to unsettling easy thinking around them. Further to this is the more theoretical, directly analytical work we do with young people. This includes skills in critical reading (looking at newspaper articles in a historical context; for instance, we undertake group readings of current *Daily Mail* editorials in the light of their view of the rise of Hitler), as well as attempting some logical analysis (we look, for example, at ways to argue for the existence of Santa Claus and then consider where the fallacies are).

Secondly, we try to teach what we call critical practice. By this we mean essentially the way that a political subject can intervene in the world around them, moderating their ambitions in line with reality, whilst not losing sight of their goals and principles. To this end, we look at various historical movements for emancipation including the African National Congress, the foundation of the British Labour movement and early feminist reformers. This strand of work also includes introducing young people to groups and individuals who are pursuing political aims in a way that we hope they will find inspiring. In addition to Palestinian and Israeli peace activists, we work with organizations like Liberty, Amnesty and Changemakers, to show young people the avenues of expression that enable them to engage politically. We try to take into account the fact that many young people are interested in, and indeed practice, arts of various kinds. So, we find it useful to embed teaching around the social and political importance of the arts in a lot of our sessions, using examples of socially conscious artists to encourage social expression from the great many artistically-talented young people that our society produces. Recently, we have begun to design and deliver programmes that, drawing on this, have focused on getting talented young people to work with professional artists to try to create some theatre, as well as attempting to build more musical ideas into this portion of our work. Critical practice, one could say, is about how to relate reasonably within a public political universe once the narrow base of identity politics has been challenged and displaced.

The third strand of our work, the inculcation of social responsibility, is the most difficult to articulate practically. The importance of this strand, especially in the light of our work with those vulnerable to violent extremism, comes from a subversion of the commonplace assumption about what drives people into the arms of such ideologies. The dominant view seems to maintain that the problem of violent extremism emerges when the terrified subject flees the unbearable weight of freedom allegedly latent in the postmodern condition for the womb-like safety of an authoritarian religio-political *Weltanschauung* (be it traditionally religious in character, racial or whatever). We would have to disagree. In fact, a number of psychologists active in the post-war period in former Yugoslavia did some interesting research on this very issue. In discussion with former paramilitaries, what struck them was the profound sense of freedom felt by those who identified themselves entirely with some supra-historical category (in this case, the racial-nation state). When someone belonged to the self-described supra-historical group, it became normal to have a complete disregard for any kind of responsibility to anyone outside the group.

You see it with those who embrace jihad, not as a classical Muslim jurisprudent would understand it, namely, as an internal struggle of faith standing in relation to a certain conception of just martial action, but as a teaching that sanctions the killing of civilians, with freedom from the constraint of more complex teaching or a sense of accountability to community. We saw it as vital to encourage the young people to regard themselves as responsible to all human beings, rather than to some narrow group based on identity. Given the difficulties of imparting such a virtue as responsibility we made the most of the fact that all our staff have backgrounds in the kind of political work that is built on social responsibility. We agreed with those who have noted it is a sign of the poverty of our age that such a term seems to bring nothing more than the self-satisfied swing of reusable carrier bags to mind. Hand in hand with a number of academics who specialized in the theory and practice of mentoring (including Margaret Alipoor at Bradford University), we have been able to sharpen up the practical implications of this position.

In short, we must distinguish between the problem of violent extremism as it is perceived and what it is in reality. People, in so far as we have seen, fall under the sway of violent political ideologies not because they are too political (understood as too focused on a principle, or on issues of race or class, or 'obsessed' with the situation in Palestine). On the contrary, they do so because they are not political enough. Our day-to-day work with vulnerable individuals has shown us that their move towards extremism is based on a lack of critical political engagement, a closing down of the political universe. In the face of this we try and support young men and women as they attempt to relate to each other in a very specific way: not as men or women, or members of specific communities, but as members of a rational political universe; as critically aware and socially responsible political subjects.

From Bradford, we move into different territory as contributors continue to reflect on the engagement between the Church of England and Islam, particularly in the light of what it means to be hospitable. Rachel Mann explores the fraught ground of free speech and offence as she considers a festival in Liverpool that received a hostile reception from local Muslims. She argues for the importance of satire to a healthy society, and offers some thoughts on the place of the church in society, and the nature of Jesus Christ. Ian Wallis works in a parish in Sheffield where there is the possibility that a local redundant church might become a mosque. For him, this raised questions about the nature of hospitality, being a host and guest in today's British society. What it means to be a host, and guest, is central to Catriona Laing's essay on scriptural reasoning, as she has experienced it in Cambridge, Bradford and London. The final chapter is an account of Judith, a sister in an enclosed order in Oxford called Sisters of the Love of God. She developed a warm relationship with a local Muslim fish and chip shop owner, which led to their praying together. She describes how her own faith was expanded by the experience.

7

The Importance of Offence: Satire, the Church of England and Islam

Rachel Mann

Mindful of the social and political background that has shaped her as a poet, as a citizen and as a priest, Rachel Mann reaches towards the theological grounding for her conviction that offence is an important part of honest encounter. Part of what she does is to consider the implications of offence for a British culture too swamped by fear and suspicion to be able to venture the intimate critique of satire (or other forms of risky representation) and too defined by crude perceptions of particular interest groups within the nation to maintain a healthy sense either of multiple difference or shared citizenship. But underpinning all she writes here is her perception that in the person of Jesus we find someone so generous, and so radically unafraid, that he is able to absorb and transform all offence into the abundant and holy risen life which follows the offence of the Cross.

Every second year there is a major festival of public art in Liverpool, the Liverpool Biennial.[1] This includes major pieces of new artwork, displayed around the city in prominent public spaces. In 2004 this festival included a piece by Yoko Ono, very well known in the city as the widow of John Lennon, entitled *My Mummy was Beautiful*. This was a series of full colour photographs of her mother's body from her breasts to her thighs. This artwork was reproduced and displayed in different places around the city, including John Lennon Airport, where it was to be viewed as one went up to the departure area, a concourse that is also the way to the interfaith chapel. The artwork was also displayed on lamp-posts in the city centre. Rupert Hoare was the dean of the Anglican cathedral and chair of the Council of Faiths at the time and therefore found himself involved in controversy, especially as some Muslim protesters wanted to express their disapproval by joining a Council of Faiths walk through the city. He refused them, because, he said, 'in my view that would have been to alter the purpose of our annual interfaith walk to the various worship centres of the Council of Faiths, which was to be an act of witness to interfaith collaboration, rather than a protest march'. He was asked to arrange a meeting between members of the Muslim community and the Director of the Liverpool Biennial. Rupert Hoare continues:

> I met with him; he agreed to come to the home of a leading Muslim in the city. I took him, with a colleague, to this man's home, where the meeting took place, with a number of Muslim people, some, if I remember aright, having come up from London. The meeting was respectful; the Muslim hosts gave us their normal excellent hospitality, and both sides were able to put their points of view. The Director did not back down from his decision to display the artwork, but listened attentively to the Muslims as they spelled out their disapproval of this artwork being displayed in public places. This was on two grounds: it offended against women's dignity and modesty, and it made it impossible for men to obey the prophet's injunction to lower their eyes to avoid looking at a woman's naked body. The only way they could avoid doing so, would have been not to go into the city centre (or the airport) during the course of the biennial. This would have made the city centre a 'no go' area for a part of the population of Liverpool. They would not have objected in the same way if the artwork had been displayed indoors in an exhibition area into which one could freely decide to go, but did not need to go.

The discussion also explored freedom of expression, the tradition in

Western art of nudity in paintings and sculptures, and the distinction between art for the sake of eroticism and art for the sake of beauty. It was maintained that the artwork in question was to be seen as beautiful rather than erotic.

There are a number of interesting issues here. Rupert Hoare quite casually talks of 'the Muslim community' and meeting at the home of a 'leading Muslim'. Hoare's use of those terms show how unthinking they have become. The presumption is for homogeneity rather than the truth that Islam is a fascinatingly and excitingly diverse faith with all variants represented in the UK including in our large cities. This 'incident' shows the friction that is generated by differing priorities in a plural society. The Biennial team demonstrated courage in defending the art and the free expression it represented.

I am, as a result of my work as a poet, in conversation with, and work alongside, people of many faiths and none. I have participated in workshop situations with Muslim, atheist, agnostic and Jewish poets where artistically ambitious poetry has been shared, whether of an erotic, explicit, foul-mouthed, even violent nature; sacred texts and figures have frequently been parodied or toyed with (often from the Old Testament scriptures held sacred by all three Abrahamic faiths). Perhaps the sheer fact that we were *poets,* that is, people committed to art, enabled the diverse individuals in such contexts to live with, discuss, disagree about and even enjoy cultural artefacts that might easily be considered 'offensive'. It is clear to me that on a one-to-one level, engaging in the sometimes fierce exchange of ideas that happens between human equals has fostered genuine friendships, which have been fraught at times, but are real nonetheless. That is, when one sees in the eyes of the other not the representative of a group, but a bearer of 'the image', with all the complexities that go with it, real relationships have emerged. These are relationships of respect rather than tolerance, where offence happens and disagreements take place, but are not destructive. If this can happen at the personal level, then I trust it is possible elsewhere.

I have this fear: that liberal British society has become anxious about causing offence and that such anxiety generates a less interesting, less ambitious and ultimately less risky culture. My sense is that this anxiety about causing offence has crystallized around Muslims. Now, like all fears, my anxiety may be irrational and ill-formed, but it has stayed with me and requires further exploration. With such an anxiety, the prospects for true friendship, *adult* friendship as it were, becomes less promising. Friendship is about real engagement; about both parties being willing to give and receive and be genuinely changed. Adult relationships involve both affirmation and questioning – a sometimes bruising and offensive encounter. Without the prospect of a culture that permits the dangerous and potentially offensive, true hospitality seems remote. My contention in this chapter is that the church holds within itself the social and theological resources to model for others ways of taking offence well and fostering true hospitality, and that the heart of that lies in the nature of Christ.

My anxiety about the current state of society is grounded in social and personal factors. I work as a priest in a part of Manchester with a 25 per cent South Asian population and I build friendships with individuals and religious communities carefully. These communities are more nuanced than the media often allows. I know how readily some of my own congregation buy a 'Muslims are taking over our area' line and am desperate to educate folk out of that. Equally, I am aware that as a middle-class, highly-educated queer feminist I try, for good or ill, to deal with my own suspicions that Islam, in its more fundamentalist forms, is 'anti-women', 'anti-gay' and 'anti-liberty'. I remain unsure how successful I've been in doing that. And then, as a poet and critic, I am conscious of many of the artistic debates that have emerged about the appropriate limits of 'free speech' and 'artistic expression' post-9/11. My instinct, perhaps unsurprisingly, has always been to support creative free expression. This paper is the product of an honest wrestling with all these factors, desperately seeking to produce creative but honest conclusions and not give into base prejudice.

Terms like 'community cohesion' have become commonplace in recent years; 'multiculturalism' has become part of the plumbing of

Britain's social and political fabric. Like with plumbing, one tends not to be troubled by the workings of our basic concepts of multi-culturalism unless they go wrong in some way. I hope the metaphor has some attraction. This chapter emerges out of a suspicion that the conceptual or philosophical plumbing of our society may be a little broken or, at the very least, a little blocked up.[2] Specifically, I am thinking of the following significant priorities: first, the cherished, deeply-held disposition towards freedom of speech and its corollary, artistic, political and journalistic expression; and secondly, the equally significant cultural desire for protection of the vulnerable, the powerless and the marginalized. Both are valuable priorities, and both are hallmarks of open, generous societies. Neither priority is, for example, considered significant in totalitarian, fascistic states. Given the nature of our conceptual plumbing, one point of friction occurs when artistic expression causes offence to the significant 'group', and yet I wish to suggest that ambitious and true friendship holds within it the unavoidability of bruising encounter. As Kenan Malik crisply puts it, 'The giving and accepting of offence is a natural part of living in a plural world. If we want the pleasures of pluralism, we have to be grown-up enough to accept the pain too.'[3]

If that is the plumber's assessment, I want, perhaps surprisingly, to suggest that part of the plumber's solution lies in what the Church of England in its role as national church might have to offer. You could say that the Church of England represents some of the oldest and most blocked bits of our cultural plumbing; and yet somehow precisely because of this, precisely because it runs very deep, it offers a healthy way of being both authentically holy and radically friendly, and has learnt to take offence well. The national church today, more often than not, models a courteous welcome to religious and ethnic minorities as a prime religious virtue: a radical graciousness which is unafraid of what it finds offensive and damaging; which might actually welcome criticism and bruising encounters. The resources for that lie not only in how grounded it is in the 'pipework' of England, but in the very character of Christ, who both offended the world, and was God's very agent of transformation.

I need to examine and defend these potentially contentious claims. First, I am an unashamed supporter of what I've long considered one of the jewels of secular culture – the bliss of free and critical artistic self-expression. I am a child of the 1960s artistic and cultural explosion and, as both a writer and human being, I am very glad for that explosion. I take the end of 'obscenity' as an uncontested good, signifying a growing cultural maturity in Britain and making available new artistic space. The death of deference, epitomized in programmes such as *That Was The Week That Was* and other satirical work, is wholly good. Whatever one might say about the state of modern art, literature and satire, the revolution has happened. The pre-1960s era, with one or two marvellous exceptions, seems as alien to modern cultural eyes as 1950s images of vicars on bicycles. The 1960s era, of course, is rooted in earlier movements in European art like Futurism, Vorticism and Imagism and also to social moments like *fin de siècle* decadence and the 1920s *bright young things*. Whilst I have no wish to idolize the artistic freedoms which became crystallized during the 1960s, nor do I wish to say that artists should, in some romantic sense, be beyond criticism, I am inclined to say, somewhat crudely, 'free speech and expression' should be preferred to 'censorship'. Part of the attractiveness of a liberal secular society lies in its capacity to allow both the parody, satire and criticism of others' cherished views as well as of one's own.

Along with others, I'm not sure that what we have come to call 'multiculturalism' is an unalloyed good anymore. Saying this makes me feel very nervous: clearly I have no wish to add armaments to the nasty likes of the BNP. However, as noted earlier, our conceptual schemes, like our plumbing, are not damage-proof. Any political concept which becomes embedded in a culture – whether that be 'democracy', 'social contract', 'community cohesion' – gets furred up over time. Multiculturalism is no different. Kenan Malik and Emmanuel Lartey[4] argue that multiculturalism runs the risk of creating the illusion of homogenized, hermetically-sealed identity groups with which the political elites can then easily deal. From the perspective of pastoral care, Lartey's comments on multiculturalism have wide appeal: he notes that it 'fails to appreciate the complexity of culture and, worse still, overlooks the reality of individual differences within cultural groups'.[5] Fundamentally, it fails to recognize that 'every person is in some respects, (a) like all others, (b) like some others, and (c) like no other'.[6] Malik makes a plausible case for questioning UK approaches to multiculturalism, specifically in relation to a 'group' many people, both within and without, see as homogenized: Muslims.

Malik has studied the multicultural policies of councils in cities like Birmingham, London and Bradford. He suggests that after the urban violence of the early 1980s, councils imposed identities on local communities that ignored the diversity of differences of class, faith and gender within such communities. Such policies empowered so-called community leaders over the voices of diverse individuals and interest groups and 'once political power and financial resources became allocated by ethnicity, then people began to identify themselves in terms of their ethnicity, and only their ethnicity'.[7] And so, over the past 20 years, the notion of being 'a Muslim' has become a significant expression of personal and political identity. Malik offers an account of how this has emerged in such a definitive way by showing that if one is a Bangladeshi living in a deprived area of a city,

… it is difficult to get the council's attention by insisting that your area is poor or disadvantaged. But if you were to say that the Muslim community is deprived or lacking, then council coffers suddenly open up – not because the council is particularly inclined to help Muslims, but because being 'Muslim', unlike being 'poor' or 'disadvantaged', registers in the bureaucratic mind as an authentic identity. Over time, you come to see yourself as a Muslim and a Bangladeshi, not just because those identities provide you with access to power, influence and resources, but also because those identities have come to possess a social reality through receiving constant confirmation and affirmation.[8]

In common with Malik, I would argue that the notion of 'the Muslim community' is a lazy misnomer which has led in part to the radicalization of certain individuals. Multiculturalism[9] has helped to generate a less interesting, more defensive Islam, betraying its more liberal traditions by privileging the voices of self-appointed community leaders. I'd even go as far as to say that the illusion of self-defined and self-sufficient 'multicultural' communities, each operating in different spheres and, de facto at least, beyond criticism, is one of the great structural sins of early twenty-first-century Britain. It is multicultural policies, ultimately supported by all political parties, which invited people to identify themselves increasingly with specific communities for the sake of 'gaining a voice' and accessing power. In 1979, there was no such thing as 'the Muslim community'; still less was there such a thing as 'the Lesbian, Gay, Bisexual and Transgender Community' (of which, I am told, I am a member). Identity politics has been a dominant motif of the past 30 years, to the detriment of British society.[10]

So how can the church speak to this complex cultural and political situation in a way that brings hope rather than inflammation, and challenging commitment rather than politeness? The Church of England has a rich and complex relationship with 'minority communities' and, in recent times, has worked reasonably confidently to build relationships, especially between Christians and Muslims. There has been considerable energy, including in parishes where I have served, to meet, befriend and get to know local imams and Muslim groups. Much of this work has been impressive and essential, but there has been less energy within the church to wrestle theologically with how to model to other faith minorities an expansive way of living in a secular world, which doesn't understand any faith tradition well. Unfashionable though it might be, I want to suggest that the Church of England has within it the wherewithal to offer a lead to other traditions, to show others how to live well as a minority tradition and a community of faith, demonstrating how to move beyond fear towards peaceful and active participation in British society today. And at the heart of that confidence is a lack of fear of the potentially offensive.

A significant way that the church might model radical hospitality for other faith traditions lies in the area of art and free expression. But as I reflect on this, 'Islamic' reactions to 'secular' cultural and artistic freedoms and sensitivity about offence make me anxious. I perceive that in recent history, groups claiming to represent Islam have become (rather like an oversensitive child) desperate to close down criticism, especially artistic and satirical criticism, of Islamic self-identity or to stop public works of art and creativity which they perceive as 'offensive' to Islamic moral and religious sensibility. Take the 'Mohammad cartoon' scandal of 2005. In choosing this example I am not necessarily endorsing the work – the pieces are of differing quality – but use it to demonstrate the extent to which British cultural media has become self-censoring and anxious.

On 30 September 2005, *Jyllands-Posten*, a right-wing leaning Danish newspaper, published caricatures of Mohammad by 12 cartoonists under the headline 'Mohammad's Angst'. Most people take that as the starting point of the scandal that affected news and cultural media worldwide. However, what many people forget was that for at least a week very little reaction was made to the cartoons, until journalists contacted a number of imams for their responses. The cartoons had simply not registered with Muslim leaders; but once the focus was on them, Islamists quickly recognized the opportunity presented. Now, clearly there are questions here about the ethics and intentions of the journalists involved; one might appropriately criticize the journalists as *agents provocateurs*. On the other hand, in a world of free media and critical expression, taste and restraint are rarely significant virtues, whereas boundary pushing is. Thus began a controversy which generated opinion from many quarters, from Islamists to moderate Muslims, from national governments to private individuals. It assumed an international significance not seen since the Rushdie affair in 1989. The similarities between the two incidents indicate a significant fact: that neither was particularly about religion, but much more about politics. The differences between the two events, however, indicate an important shift in Western perceptions between 1989 and 2005 over matters of censorship and offence, especially to a group perceived as essentially other and as essentially homogenous – Muslims. There is little doubt that the international response to the Danish cartoons provided a telling comment on how the landscape of free speech had been reshaped since the Rushdie affair. As Kenan Malik notes:

> Once free speech had been seen as an inherent good, the fullest extension of which was a necessary condition to the elucidation of truth, the expression of moral autonomy ... In the post-Rushdie world speech became seen as inherently a problem, because it could offend as well as harm, and speech that offended could be as socially damaging as speech that harmed.[11]

In the post-Fatwa context, self-censorship has become the norm; speech is now restrained by an internalized fear of causing offence to people with deeply-held beliefs. No Fatwa was produced over the Danish cartoons – but in a sense there was no need. The West – its politicians, religious leaders, even much of its so-called self-willed media – had internalized the lesson. The West imposed its own Fatwa on itself. It had decided that 'social cohesion' (whatever that means) was worth pronouncements of self-censorship.

Church reactions were predictable and understandable and fit, in essence, the contentions made above. Interfaith vigils were held. At one such vigil, at the Stratford Street mosque in Beeston, Leeds, the Revd Neil Bishop, a Methodist minister, said: 'We are here to demonstrate our respect for one another, and say that freedom of speech needs to be exercised with compassion and respect for those things that people regard as holy.' Equally, speaking at a dinner at Mansion House, the Archbishop of Canterbury, Rowan Williams, talked of civility, that it 'is the condition of patient cooperation between strangers'. He added:

> The Western world likes to think that it is inviting other cultures into a peaceful and enlightened atmosphere of civility. But the 'strangers' invited in may well be dismayed to discover that this

peacefulness and enlightenment seems to include licence to express some very unpeaceful and unenlightened attitudes to minorities of various kinds ... Enlightened attitudes are, understandably, seen by minorities as a refusal to believe that others take their convictions seriously.

The then Bishop of Oxford, the Rt Revd Richard Harries, said that newspapers that decided not to publish the cartoons had acted wisely. He told *The Sunday Times*: 'Freedom of speech is fundamental to our society, and all religions need to be open to criticism, but this freedom needs to be exercised responsibly with a sensitivity to cultural differences.'

Williams' instinctively irenic approach is impressive, with his emphasis on civility that affords to 'the other' the respect of the citizen.[12] Civility finds its roots in the notion of 'civitas', which is grounded in Roman polity and jurisprudence. I turn to the person of Christ for something bolder. At the heart of the church is a figure who was prepared to embrace the offence and dishonour of the world even if it took him to his own death. He was utterly unafraid of the world's contempt of the Holy. Such a person, Jesus Christ, is far more significant than the 'civility' that Williams claims. Christ's willingness to embrace the humiliation of the world, as he died on the Cross, shows us a way for taking offensiveness and perceived criticism well; a way to embrace all that the world can dish out without descending into defensiveness. A confident church might even be so bold as to live that 'way of Christ' in a manner that is salutary for other minorities.[13] In short, this can embody a way of being that does not need to 'defend' the Holy.

Christ's trial and death on the Cross can be understood to address the real issue of how dangerous it is when the Holy is satirized. Despite what others might say about him[14] and what his actions have demonstrated,[15] cynical power brokers, like the High Priests, and those who governed and represented the established 'civility', like Pontius Pilate, actively humiliated Christ, the Holy One, even parodying him by calling him 'The King of the Jews'. And Christ did not fight back, but absorbed the insult. At the heart of the mystery of the Cross is Christ's lack of need for defence. To crucify the one sent by God to proclaim his kingdom is about as brutal an insult as can be delivered to God: it is the fundamental offence, but God in Christ does not respond by defending honour and reputation.

Of course, the story does not end there for Christians, in the crushed hope and brutal offence of the Cross. Resurrection follows and offers the ultimate context for the offence of the Cross. Resurrection is the ground of St Paul's profoundly boastful hope in Romans chapter 5, verse 2b: '… we boast in our hope of sharing the glory of God' (NRSV translation). The resurrection is the recovery of the language of the glory of holiness in the face of apparent failure. To put it another way, tragedy can never be the final word in any Christian narrative; the last word is Jesus Christ.

Perhaps, then, the church is a satire on the world. Samuel Wells has spoken of the church as 'an ironic parody of society, a satire on secularism'.[16] He argues that 'the Christian story amounts to a satire on the story that there is no story'.[17] I suspect he is right to talk of satire as the condition of the church. Its actions often look much like the actions of others: it does not always 'look redeemed'; it can claim no superiority of power or goodness.[18] Yet its practices, such as confession and reconciliation, baptism and Eucharist and so on, hint at a story that exposes the emptiness of the world's longings. Wells writes:

> The Church is the cuckoo in the nest, on others' territory, a resident alien … [it] inhabits the same space as the rest of society, but has a perspective that makes some of the nostrums of that society seem absurd. [It] makes no claims to superiority or seclusion: it simply operates with a different timescale from the rest of society. For the Church, that is the eschatological perspective.[19]

It also liberates it from the need to 'defend' the Holy from all-comers.

So runs the Christian story of the Holy. Clearly, in its details, it is not the Islamic or the Jewish or the Sikh story.[20] But surely it signifies a truth that all faith traditions can dare to affirm out of their own theological resources: that faith is essentially a satire on secularism, on the story that there is no story. Tempted as any of us may be to 'defend God', God does not need it. Perhaps the Christian story has the means to make this point most clearly and as the story of the Liverpool Biennial arts festival illustrated, perhaps the Church of England is in the best position to model it creatively for others in the cultural context of Britain today.

Notes

1 I am grateful for conversations I've had with my colleague and friend, Bishop Rupert Hoare, who was intimately involved in teasing out some of the issues raised by this event. I recognize that this example is in many respects based on anecdotal evidence, but is interesting because it is focused on a perspective that was seeking to hold the ring.

2 The notion of 'philosophical plumbing' was most famously developed in Mary Midgley's article of the same name in A. Phillips Griffiths (ed.), *The Impulse to Philosophise* (Cambridge: CUP, 1992). Sarah Coakley also makes use of the 'drain' metaphor in Sam Wells and Sarah Coakley (eds), *Praying for England* (London: Continuum, 2008).

3 Kenan Malik, *From Fatwa to Jihad* (London: Atlantic, 2009), p. 172.

4 Though admittedly Lartey is commenting on the notion of multicultural pastoral counselling; however, his comments still have weight in a more specifically political context, not least because he is conscious of the political dimensions of pastoral care.

5 E. Lartey, *In Living Color: An Intercultural Approach to Pastoral Care and Counseling*, 2nd edn (London: Jessica Kingsley Publishers, 2003), p. 170.

6 Lartey, op. cit., p. 171.

7 Malik, op. cit., p. 68.

8 Malik, op. cit., p. 69.

9 Or what Amartya Sen, the Nobel-prize-winning economist, has called 'plural monoculturalism' – a policy driven by the myth that society is made up of a series of distinct, uniform cultures which dance around one another.

10 One of the questions raised against this discomfort about talking of the 'Muslim community' or 'LGBT community' is: 'What else are we supposed to say?' I wish I had some ready-made response; the linguistic battle may have already been lost. My desire is multifold: first, for these casually used phrases to become 'sensitized'; that is, for users of them to become fully conscious of how limited their purchase is; second, I desire greater degrees of nuance in our talk of communities. If 'Muslim community', then why not 'Sunni' or 'Shia' communities? Why not 'Salafi' or 'Deobandi' or 'Baralwi' communities? Perhaps as our media and social world matures this may become possible. Ultimately, changes in terms – towards something more nuanced – will depend on many factors. These will include choices made by media

organizations, critical rejection of the terms by individuals and groups, and the genuine growth of intercultural trust and friendship.

11 Malik, op. cit., p. 151.

12 Though I am less convinced by his claim that 'The Western world likes to think that it is inviting other cultures into a peaceful and enlightened atmosphere of civility'; the Western world does like to think of itself as enlightened, but one element of that is a culture of critique and a free press. This 'civility' is dangerous and hard-edged; Western 'civility' is no longer, if it ever was, a nice 'gentlemen's club'.

13 And despite whatever spin doctors and censuses might suggest, the Church of England – in terms of active participation – is a minority; a privileged and still influential one, but a minority nonetheless.

14 Definitively, St Peter – 'You are the Messiah, the Holy One of God.'

15 Miraculous healings, raising from the dead, etc.

16 Samuel Wells, *Transforming Fate into Destiny: The Theological Ethics of Stanley Hauerwas* (Carlisle: Paternoster, 1998), p. 171.

17 Ibid.

18 Ibid

19 Op. cit., p.172

20 At one level, the very idea of 'God' being crucified is 'offensive' to Jewish and Muslim sensibilities.

8

Giving Place: Exploring Christian Hospitality

Ian Wallis

It is appropriate that Ian Wallis begins his account of how a redundant church did not quite become a mosque with a reflection on the Eucharist. The Eucharist is not only a fitting metaphor for the hospitality where host is guest and guest is host, but has a history which begins with radical generosity but quickly becomes conditional, a sign of belonging. Wallis ends with the receding of the mosque initiative, the huge and probably insuperable difficulties which will prevent the change of use to a prayer space that is right for today's predominantly Muslim residents of Broomhall. But what Ian traces is a process of growing trust and intimacy as the possibility is considered, with the space sought and offered locally. Like the spiritual feast which is the Eucharist, St Silas's in this chapter becomes a place of spiritual hospitality where the place of guest and of host is shared, at moments transcending the incompleteness and division of fallen social affairs, which is where we must usually live.

'Do not neglect to show hospitality (*philoxenias*) to strangers, for thereby some have entertained (*xenisantes*) angels unawares' (Hebrews 13.2; RSV). This biblical exhortation, preserved within a letter addressed to an oppressed community (cf. 10.32-39; 12.1-11), reminds us that the practice of hospitality has been a defining expression of Christian faith from the outset. Each week, church congregations appropriate this inheritance through celebrations of the Eucharist, although ritual and (often) restricted participation disguise its origins within the radical hospitality of Jesus' open-tabled commensality. This dimension of his kingdom ministry is evident from the outset when, recruiting apprentice disciples, his practice proved controversial:

> And as he sat at dinner in Levi's house, many tax collectors and sinners were also sitting with Jesus and his disciples – for there were many who followed him. When the scribes of the Pharisees saw that he was eating with sinners and tax collectors, they said to his disciples, 'Why does he eat with tax collectors and sinners?' (Mark 2.15-16; NRSV, here and henceforth)

Yet this is only one instance of a characteristic trope in which Jesus draws criticism from various Jewish denominations. For example, he refuses to fast (Mark 2.18-19), gathers food on the Sabbath (Mark 2.23-27) and fails to observe purity regulations (Mark 7.1-7).

From this perspective, the *Last* Supper, an alternative appellation for Holy Communion or the Eucharist, points us in the right direction by encouraging us to interpret and, indeed, to perform Christian hospitality in the light not only of what would follow (that is, Jesus' crucifixion and resurrection), but also of what went before (that is, Jesus' ministry). It seems that prior to Jesus uttering, 'Do this in remembrance of me' (Luke 22.19; 1 Corinthians 11.25), he was already being remembered as someone who kept bad company and hosted feasts of abundance: 'a glutton and a drunkard, a friend of tax collectors and sinners!' ... 'And all ate and were filled; and they took up twelve baskets full of broken pieces and of the fish. Those who had eaten the loaves numbered five thousand men' (Luke 7.34; Mark 6.42-44). This was a reputation that was all the more remarkable given the austere living conditions characterizing village life in first-century Galilee.

Hebrews 13.2 also reminds us of the reciprocal dynamics embedded within the practice of hospitality in which the roles of 'host' and 'guest' are not static, but oscillate among participants as various gifts are offered and received. Significantly, this dimension, reflected in the semantics of the biblical languages (for example, *xenos* denotes a 'stranger' in Matthew 25.35, but a 'host' in Romans 16.23), is enshrined within the archetypal gospel narrative celebrating Jesus' continuing presence, namely the Emmaus encounter where disciples extend hospitality to a 'stranger' who subsequently communicates Christ: 'When he was at the table with them, he took bread, blessed and broke it, and gave it to them. Then their eyes were opened, and they recognized him; and he vanished from their sight' (Luke 24.30-31; cf. 24.13-35).

What is equally striking is that although roles can be reversed, they still need to be performed, highlighting a sacrificial economy implicit within hospitality. Where nothing is owned, nothing can be offered or received; instead, all are entitled to a fair share, as the demand of rights replaces the opportunities of grace. One wonders, then, how hospitality functions within a community where 'no one claimed private ownership of any possessions, but everything they owned was held in common' (Acts 4.32; cf. 2.43-47).

Our discussion so far has related instances of what is a central, although often implicit, biblical theme, namely that creation is itself an expression of divine hospitality in which creatures are invited to participate. In the case of human beings, this extends beyond mere creaturely existence to cooperation in divine creation – an invitation articulated in terms of the Genesis creation myths:

So God created humankind in his image, in the image of God he created them; male and female he created them. God blessed them, and God said to them, 'Be fruitful and multiply, and fill the earth and subdue it; and have dominion over the fish of the sea and over the birds of the air and over every living thing that moves upon the earth.' (Genesis 1.27-28; cf. 2.15-20)

Hospitality is also articulated in terms of election and covenant through which recipients of grace are commissioned and resourced to extend hospitality to others in God's name, as guest becomes host: 'I will make of you a great nation, and I will bless you, and make your name great, so that you will be a blessing ... and in you all the families of the earth shall be blessed' (Genesis 12.2-3). This is an insight with far-reaching implications for an established church or a prominent faith-tradition within a particular time and place! Interestingly, no sooner does Abraham and Sarah's practice of hospitality commence, providing welcome, refreshment and sustenance for travellers at the oaks of Mamre, than the tables are turned with the announcement of good news by one of the guests – 'I will surely return to you in due season, and your wife Sarah shall have a son' (Genesis 18.10) – thereby supplying further evidence of hospitality's reciprocal nature.

The biblical witness to the practice of hospitality, however, is far from unambiguous. For example, claiming by divine right a tract of land inhabited by other people appears to be a predatory and supremely inhospitable act (cf. Leviticus 20.24). Equally, the observance of cultural protocols could have horrific consequences, epitomized in the readiness of both Lot and the unnamed resident of Gibeah to hand over their daughters to be sexually abused in order to protect their house-guests from harm (Genesis 19.1-11; Judges 19.22-30). Less extreme are those instances where the motivation for offering hospitality is morally bankrupt, for instance when Jacob prepares a meal for Esau in order to acquire his birthright (Genesis 25.29-34) or to deceive his father and obtain his elder brother's blessing (Genesis 27.1-29). Jesus also warns against compromising hospitality through an ulterior motive. For example, a host may invite as table-guests only those in a position to reciprocate (Luke 14.12-14) or invite someone for the purpose of humiliation (Luke 7.39, 44-46). Equally, guests may exploit hospitality by disregarding invitations (Matthew 22.1-6; Luke 14.16-21), seeing an invitation as an opportunity for self-promotion (Luke 14.7-11) or something worse: 'Truly I tell you, one of you will betray me, one who is eating with me' (Mark 14.18).

Yet, for all this, much of Jesus' ministry can be interpreted as a hosting of God's presence through enabling those whom he encountered to experience some aspect of the divine life embedded within personal experience. Both his 'feasting not fasting' approach to ministry and his readiness to feed and find fellowship with a variegated cross-section of humanity belong to the bedrock of our earliest remembrances of Jesus (cf. Mark 2.15-20; 6.35-44; Luke 7.33-35; Matthew 11.18-19). It seems that such radical hospitality embodied much that was central to his vision and vocation: welcome and acceptance, forgiveness and reconciliation, joy and celebration, sustenance and satisfaction, giving and receiving, generosity and thanksgiving, trust and friendship, sharing and consideration, equality and justice, belonging and responsibility.

It is this legacy that Jesus entrusted to his followers at the Last Supper and, judging from the New Testament and other early Christian literature, it is one that was embraced, at least partially, although not without difficulty. For one thing, sharing hospitality across ethnicities proved particularly problematic with some Jewish Christians unwilling to eat with their Gentile counterparts (cf. Acts 10.9-16; 11.1-18; 15.28-29; Galatians 2.11-14). Equally, there were moral sensitivities around food that had been sacrificed on pagan altars (as much was in first-century Greco-Roman conurbations) before being used within a Christian context (cf. 1 Corinthians 8.1-13; 10.23-33). Further, shared meals were not always characterized by the spirit of their founder, with hosts using the Lord's Supper to reinforce social divisions and hierarchies rather than to subvert them (cf. 1 Corinthians 11.17-22). It also appears that some recipients of Christian hospitality took advantage of the generosity of others, seeing this as an opportunity for indolence (2 Thessalonians 3.6-13). Significantly, by the end of the first century, Jesus' open table of inclusive commensality had given way to conditional participation, whether based upon a willingness to work (2 Thessalonians 3.6-13), spiritual discernment (1 Corinthians 11.27-34) or a readiness to embrace the Christian way through initiation: 'Let no one eat or drink of your thanksgiving [meal] save those who have been baptized in the name of the Lord, since the Lord has said concerning this, "Do not give what is holy to the dogs"' (Didache 9.5).

♦ ♦ ♦ ♦ ♦

What follows is an account of an ongoing episode in one Anglican church's attempt to bear witness among Muslims to Jesus' radical practice of hospitality viewed in its widest sense. The neighbourhood of Broomhall is on the western side of Sheffield, framed by major roads and characterized by a broad range of housing stock, from substantial Victorian piles through multiple occupancy terraces to high-rise flats. Many of the former are currently occupied by Sheffield Hallam University, with a substantial student population in the neighbourhood. Thirty years ago, Broomhall supported a thriving 'red light' district which has gradually relocated to another part of the city. During the same period, there has been a substantial influx of asylum seekers and economic migrants, creating an ethnically diverse community – a trend which shows little sign of abating. According to official statistics, approximately 6,500 people live in Broomhall. In 2001, the percentage who were black and minority ethnic (BME) was 36 per cent; by 2006 it had risen to 67 per cent and now is generally thought to be significantly higher. In 2008, for example, the percentage of BME children from Broomhall attending primary schools was 80 per cent. By far the largest number of these are Somali, although many other ethnicities are represented. Broomhall is recognized as presenting a number of challenges with respect to social cohesion and criminality as well as to educational attainment and access to training and employment. It is ranked 33rd out of Sheffield's most deprived neighbourhoods.

In 1998, the benefice of Broomhall ceased to exist, the parish church of St Silas was closed and the geographical area of the living subsumed within adjacent parishes, predominantly Broomhill. It is fair to say that although only one letter separates them, the neighbourhoods of Broomhall and Broomhill are miles apart. To a certain extent this is due to being separated by one of the busiest routes into Sheffield, but more significantly because Broomhill is rapidly becoming a campus for Sheffield University, incorporating not only faculties, central administration and services, but also teaching hospitals and a burgeoning student village. Add to this a number of private schools and a large comprehensive, all of which are predominantly populated by the children of students and staff residing outside the parish, and you end up with a highly-educated, well-resourced and upwardly-mobile concentration of humanity who are 'passing through' and, as a consequence, have little reason or opportunity to invest in the broader community in which they find themselves for a season. One measure of this is the 'town and gown' tension between indigenous natives and resident aliens. Quite simply, this is a different world than that of Broomhall.

My appointment to St Mark's, Broomhill (significantly, Broomhall does not appear in the title of the benefice), in 2009 was something of a homecoming. I had grown up in Sheffield, attending schools and university all within the parish, before commencing a career in IT with a family-owned company. Returning 20 years later, the changes, especially in Broomhall, were pronounced. Before leaving, I had served on the board of management of a thriving YMCA based in a purpose-built complex located there; the Robert Winston building, as it now is, houses Sheffield Hallam's department of Health and Wellbeing. 'What of the wellbeing of Sheffield YMCA?' I wondered.

In 2006, the board of the YMCA acquired St Silas, the derelict, redundant church building at the heart of Broomhall, with the intention of converting it into a community-services hub, including a medical practice, dentist, pharmacy and optician as well as a worship area and function rooms, which was to be the jewel in the crown of Sheffield Council's multimillion 'Broomhall Cosmopolitan' scheme. Unfortunately, some of the prospective stakeholders decided to locate elsewhere, the overall project faltered, and in 2009 the church and vicarage were put on the market once more, as Sheffield YMCA refocused its activities.

By now St Silas was not only an eyesore, but also a bone of contention. Initially, this surfaced in relation to the vicarage. A local forum had facilitated the setting up of a youth council and identified grants for purchasing this property to establish a youth centre that would be run primarily by young people. However, not all parents in the vicinity were comfortable with this development and, as a consequence, decided to withdraw their children from the youth forum, thereby reducing its community representation, which was a prerequisite to securing funding. The youth centre fell through.

After a number of months in post, I recognized that St Silas was becoming a stage on which various neighbourhood tensions were being acted out. Equally, although it was a redundant church owned by a third party, some residents still identified it with the Church of England. For them, at least, it was our presence in the area that communicated absence. It spoke of a Christianity that was not 'at home' and, what is more, seemed reticent to let anybody else take up residence either. This was truer than some people realized in that, although the YMCA owned the property, a covenant restricting usage was in place which could only be changed with the consent of the Bishop of Sheffield and, depending on what was being proposed, the Church Commissioners.

Violence and unrest in Broomhall during 2008 resulted in the establishment of another consultative forum known as the Group of Groups (GoG) on which representatives from all community organizations were entitled to sit, along with community police officers, ward councillors and other public servants. My first meeting, shortly after arriving, was an unsettling occasion. The animosity and lack of trust were palpable, with recriminations filling the airwaves and a singular lack of will even to listen to one another, much less to cooperate with one another. On leaving the meeting, I inadvertently found myself walking through an outdoor truce gathering of rival gangs brokered by a local Muslim youth worker commanding respect. One teenager was openly brandishing a machete; goodness knows what weaponry was concealed in the tracksuit bottoms of others. It was a courageous initiative that thankfully passed without incident, although it would take a drive-by shooting shortly afterwards, leaving one dead and others wounded, to bring warring parties to their senses.

The following GoG meetings were no less fractious, but no less honest either. Participants expressed their fears, prejudices and aspirations, which gradually engendered a kind of sympathy born of vulnerability, embracing those who exposed what was on their mind as well as those who felt exposed as a consequence. This yielded the most unlikely of alliances. On one occasion, a property developer presented his proposals for St Silas. A sale had been agreed and an architect instructed. The former church would be converted into student accommodation. At the mention of the 's-word', Somalis, Afro-Caribbeans, Iranians and whites forgot their differences and gathered behind a common enemy: 'No way, there are too many students in the vicinity already!' The property developer left the meeting, shaken by the strength of opposition, and subsequently withdrew his offer.

All this only strengthened my conviction that St Silas should serve the community once more. I shared as much at the next GoG and was encouraged to discover those of similar outlook. We agreed to meet separately and explore possibilities. One option soon emerged. This part of Sheffield is home to many of Islamic faith, but is poorly served by places for them to worship. Could St Silas become one such place? A number of local Muslims believed so and were actively exploring this option. Initially, this puzzled me. Why would followers of Mohammad wish to worship in a Christian shrine? Would Sharia permit such an extraordinary development? Debating questions such as these together has been, I think, a source of mutual enrichment as we have gained a greater appreciation of each other's religious heritage. Equally, we have grown in trust and respect.

I have been struck by the commitment of these Somali Muslims to create sacred space in their community in which to pray and, equally, to extend hospitality to the residents at large. To the best of my knowledge, the cost of purchase, renovation and reordering would be met by the Muslims themselves, who have organized into a consti-tuted group and made an offer for the church and vicarage which has been accepted. Equally, I have been encouraged by their willingness to consult. A case in point occurred around the preparation of an initial proposal outlining future use for St Silas which was to be submitted to the Bishop of Sheffield. To my surprise, I was invited to comment on the initial and subsequent versions. This presented me with a dilemma. Was this offer a token gesture to secure the support of the local vicar or a genuine invitation to contribute to the planning process? And, either way, if I wished to maintain good relations and bona fides, did I dare to do anything other than register my appreciation for being consulted and offer my support for what was being proposed? I thought back to those early acrimonious GoG meetings when fear and suspicion were transcended as sound relationships began to be forged through honest, costly encounter. The current situation demanded nothing less. My response, in each case, was courteous yet robust. Some of my recommendations were readily accommodated, others not, and one continues to be debated. Plans included a prayer hall for exclusive use by Muslims as well as a range of community amenities (for example, meeting/class rooms, crèche, coffee shop, function hall, health and fitness suite), but there was no prayer space for members of other faith traditions.

This struck me as a glaring omission for a number of reasons. For one thing, the idea of Christians being prevented from praying in a former church seemed incongruous. For another, if the intention was for St Silas to be accessible to the whole community then this would be an important facility. But, most of all, such a prayer space would be an acknowledgement by the new hosts of St Silas of the hospitality extended to them in the first instance. From what I can gather, this proposal precipitated considerable debate among Somalis, revealing differences of opinion and approach – traditionalists, liberals and progressives; consenters and dissenters – demonstrating that Muslims are no more homogenous than Christians. What it hasn't apparently done, however, is compromise relationships.

It would be less than honest to pretend that negotiations have been anything other than an exercise of walking on thin ice. But, there again, transformative encounter does not take place within the detached corridors of theoretical contemplation, but in the risk-drenched miasma engendered by passionate believers daring to explore together how they can remain faithful to their own convictions without diminishing the opportunity of others to be likewise. Within this climate the dynamics of hospitality come to life, creating gracious space and possibilities for mutual enrichment hitherto unimaginable – as, in this case, one community of faith contemplates entrusting its sacred space to another who contemplates offering to share it in response. Through all this I have come to recognize that gifts cannot be given, only offered. Why? Because giving and receiving constitute a relationship of mutuality and recognition in which both donor and recipient need to participate knowingly and voluntarily.

Manifestly, permitting Muslims to worship in a redundant church raises significant theological and pastoral issues. I have been informed that no restrictive covenant on a redundant Church of England church has ever been varied to permit its use in this way. For this reason what is in effect a local matter – a parish priest helping parishioners find somewhere to pray – carries far-reaching ramifications requiring broad consultation. How would this development be viewed by the parish as a whole, or ecumenically, or within the deanery, the diocese, the House of Bishops, the General Synod, or the Anglican Communion? Discussions with the Bishop of Sheffield and Church Commissioners confirmed the magnitude of what was being proposed and the unlikelihood of permission being granted. Such an unprecedented expression of hospitality, it was stressed (although not in these terms), could only be supported after wide consultation and careful consideration within the decision-making structures of the Church of England, rather than in response to a particular pastoral need.

This sounds plausible, responsible, even wise; but is it hospitable? Interestingly, according to the author of Acts, the incorporation of Gentiles within the Christian community (that is, being hospitable to non-Jewish followers of Jesus) resulted from the witness of persons (for example, Cornelius) in whom the Holy Spirit was incontrovertibly present (Acts 10-11, 15). It was the embodiment of the issue which provided the context for theological reflection and ecclesial discernment. To my mind, few matters relating to persons are real until they acquire a face. The question of whether redundant churches should be used for Muslim prayer is a very different question from whether a group of Somali parishioners seeking somewhere to pray should be allowed to use St Silas. This is because hospitality is not practised in abstraction. Nor is it without sacrifice. It entails, rather, an (unconditional?) offering of the self for its own sake (cf. Luke 14.12-14).

Further, giving permission for Muslims to pray in a redundant church would conspicuously relate Christianity to Islam and vice versa. Would it be viewed as a relationship of equality or disparity, of mutuality or conquest? Would it erode the distinctiveness of each religion or represent a decline into relativism? Would it not be, at best, confusing, and, at worst, misleading for worship by one religious tradition to take place in a building reflecting another? These questions inevitably elicit a broad response – reason enough, it could be argued, for maintaining the status quo.

At the time of writing, it seems unlikely that the name of Allah will ever be invoked in St Silas. However, whilst recognizing why this should be the case, I cannot dislodge the following question from my mind: shouldn't Christians who readily follow a Jew and host the Hebrew Bible within their canon, be hospitable within a building they no longer need (or own) to the offering of worship by members of a monotheistic tradition that recognizes their founder, accommodates him within its scriptures and venerates him as a prophet?

The fifth (2009) edition of the *Code of Recommended Practice* for the Pastoral Measure 1983 introduces the 'Suitable Alternative Uses' for redundant churches section with the following clause:

Central to the Christian faith is the unique revelation of God in Jesus Christ and the restoration of humankind's relationship with God through Christ. Any consideration of suitable alternative uses must be placed in this context. Moreover, ecclesiastical buildings and consecrated places bear enduring public witness to the faith and values of the Christian community. (11.9)

Shouldn't our confidence in God's expansive and all-sufficient hospitality in Christ extend to sharing holy ground with the children of Abraham?

9

Scriptural Reasoning

Catriona Laing

In her narrative of the experience of Scriptural Reasoning in three different contexts, Catriona Laing allows us to see some of the edginess and vulnerability which must go with sharing, discussing and comparing insights on the sacred scriptures of the three 'religions of the Book': Judaism, Christianity and Islam. In the course of her chapter we learn that the common conventions of academic discourse, or the trust and goodwill which goes with a shared civic context, make it much easier for participants to engage with each other and to avoid unfruitfully dogmatic clashes in the interpretative process. Without prior shared ground, SR becomes a much more problematic and fragile exercise. Catriona concludes that SR must flower out of, and then nourish, a wider shared life; and she holds that, when these conditions are met, the experience is indeed both healing and enriching.

Cambridge

It is Wednesday evening and after a long day of lectures, deadlines and faculty meetings we gather in the wood-panelled parlour of the Cambridge Union Society for the last Scriptural Reasoning session of term. I am exhausted and rather wish I was heading home for a good evening's telly rather than challenging intellectual engagement with the Holy Scriptures of Islam, Judaism and Christianity. However, the buzz in the air and the array of faces that have become real friends over the past five years quickly override any longing for *MasterChef* or *Spooks*. Alice, our convenor this evening, suggests we begin. Tonight's theme is hospitality.

'So who are the men?' Hoda asks. Hannah has just finished her introduction to the Jewish passage, Genesis 18:1-16, and the visit of the three men to Abraham and Sarah. Knowing glances shoot between the Christians. 'It's obvious!' says David. There is a slightly awkward pause as he remembers that this scripture is Jewish as well as Christian. He continues a little more reticently, 'Well for me, this passage is a wonderful affirmation of a Trinitarian God. This is God the Father, Son and Holy Spirit visiting Abraham by the oaks of Mamre.' 'Yes,' Emma adds, 'I'm always reminded of that painting called the *Trinity* by Rublev.' 'Yes, but wasn't it originally called 'The hospitality of Abraham and Sarah?' Hannah asks. We park the question of the identity of the visitors for the time being and move into a discussion of host and guest. 'But who is the guest and who is the host in this story?' Alice asks. 'Isn't it obvious?' Saleem replies. 'The guests are the three men.' 'But WHO ARE THE MEN?' Hoda interrupts, and the room collapses into laughter.

Ahmad, a PhD student working on Ibn Arabi, attempts a more theological answer: 'God seems to be the guest here.' 'But that means Abraham is *seeing* God. How does that work?' Saleem, who is the local imam, asks. Alice is confused: 'If Abraham as host is guiding God as guest, what does that say about humankind's relationship with God? Do we guide God?' 'Well, isn't the host also guided by his guest?' someone suggests.

My mind wanders from the conversation around the table. In many ways this is a fitting analogy for Scriptural Reasoning itself. We are both guests and hosts: guests to the scriptures of the other traditions and hosts to our own. It is this blurring of boundaries between guest and host that makes SR a constructive framework for inter-religious encounter. We feel a sense of ownership at the same time as feeling vulnerable: fear and friendship.

We move on to the Christian passage. We are reading John 12:1-9. 'This passage makes me quite angry,' Maya, a rabbi from the reformed synagogue, tells us. 'Jesus just seems so arrogant and self-centred.

Telling them not to give to the poor; it's distasteful. He's sitting there while Mary wipes his feet with her hair! Isn't it rather indulgent and erotic?' 'Wait a minute!' Ahmad intervenes. 'This is God here, not any old guy whose feet she is anointing.' 'I know,' I say, 'but what is this teaching us about hospitality? On one level, Mary is showing real hospitality, but on another, Jesus is not being hospitable to the poor in his midst.' Alice cuts in: 'My sense in these texts is that hospitality is about God, *for* God. It's not about hospitality to our fellow humans; it is about how *we respond* to God's love and hospitality for us. I think the Abraham story helps us understand this.' 'Yes,' Clara, a Muslim convert, concurs: 'This is a precious moment. Mary has realized that. In the presence of God she is giving herself completely to him. Hospitality becomes a form of worship.' Maya interrupts: 'Perhaps it does in the Qur'anic text we looked at where you give to the poor and you offer hospitality. That could be a form of worship. But in the gospel here, it's not like that. There is no hospitality being shown.' 'I hear what you're saying,' Ahmad turns to Maya, 'but there is no real equivalent in the Qur'an because we never address God in human form. As I said, this isn't any old person; this is God incarnate. She is sitting at the feet of God incarnate. That's huge.'

I feel a smile creep across my face. It *is* huge, but even more huge for me is that my Muslim friend is explaining a passage from the Christian gospel that I have always found particularly difficult to a Jewish woman in the room.

Some of my earliest memories of times spent with Muslim friends have little to do with reading scripture together. Despite growing up in the Middle East, I don't think I had ever sat down to study a passage from the Qur'an before reading theology at university. My experiences of Islam as a young person involved occasions like the time a group of us, teenage expatriates and Arabs, set out for the desert outside Riyadh in search of a safe place to hold a birthday party. We were on a quest for a place where our mixed gathering of boys and girls could socialize together safe from the prying eye of the *mutawa'een*, Saudi Arabia's religious police. But it was foolish to think they wouldn't find us. Even in our desert shack Saudi religious law applied. The holy Qur'an, they told us, forbids mixed gatherings amongst people who are not related. Threats were issued, our non-segregated party was quickly broken up and we were sent home. Such was my encounter with Islam as a British person negotiating my teenage years in the Muslim world.

Notwithstanding hostile engagements with Saudi police, my abiding impression of Islam was as the religion of some of my closest friends. My memories were of good, faithful people who had welcomed me into their world with a warmth of hospitality that any visitor to the Middle East will have encountered at some point. Nonetheless I had never sat down and thought about how their holy scripture connected word and world in the way that I often tried to think about my own scriptures. Reading the Qur'an with this group in Cambridge has awakened me to the rich tradition of faith and practice that stands at the heart of Islam. I no longer find it easy to avoid the conversations and questions I used to eschew when living in the Arab world because I was afraid of causing offence or opening a can of worms that was best kept shut. Scriptural Reasoning has provided a context through which I can begin to have those conversations.

Our Cambridge session is over, leaving a trail of unanswered questions and unfinished sentences in its wake. We discuss the next session. 'I'd like to add a passage from Isaiah,' Peter says. 'The New Testament passage reminds me of Isaiah 58; I think it would be fun to read them together.' This is SR at its best. The scriptures are selecting each other to the point where our study of the New Testament inspires one of the Jewish readers to look more closely at another part of his holy texts. Professor David Ford, one of the first Christians to join Scriptural Reasoning in the early 1990s, refers to the endlessly generative nature of scripture. He writes of the 'double-depth' achieved through reading one's scriptures with members of another faith tradition. It is a study that takes you deeper into your own scriptures whilst simultaneously taking you deeply into the study of the scriptures of another tradition.

Scriptural Reasoning: beginnings

Scriptural Reasoning began over 20 years ago when a group of Jewish scholars in America, frustrated by the lack of dialogue between the philosophers and the text scholars, began to read scripture together. Their study drew on both modern philosophy and the Talmudic tradition. In this exercise they found a way of being attentive to contemporary issues by going deeply into their tradition and holy texts. The practice turned 'inter-religious' when some Christian theologians who had witnessed the lively arguments joined the group and brought the New Testament with them. They were later joined by Muslims and have continued to meet biannually in America and in Britain for the past 15 years. Today Scriptural Reasoning groups are meeting in several different countries across four continents.

SR is so simple: Muslims, Christians and Jews gather together to study passages of scripture selected around a common theme such as 'family', 'debt' or 'Abraham'. The Jewish origins of the practice remain an important feature of SR. Disagreement and argument are part of rabbinical prayer; a gift perhaps that the Christian and Muslim traditions can inherit from Judaism. Part of the grace of SR is learning to read our scriptures in new ways. This can mean finding the freedom to disagree with each other and our scriptures in constructive ways. A spirit of openness is vital. Scholars have described the tense of reading SR as that of the optative, the conditional, or the subjunctive. We are encouraged to move away from reading scripture in a manner dominated by the grammar of imperatives and indicatives that leave no room for questions. We look for the 'let us', the 'what ifs', the 'maybes', and the 'coulds' buried within our scriptures.

Bradford

We are sitting in Foezul's sitting room in Bradford. It is a cold Monday evening in March and 12 of us have gathered to read scripture together. Mounira, who is presenting the Muslim text tonight, has just read a passage from the Qur'an. She felt it addressed the topic of parenting, our chosen theme for this session:

Thy Lord hath decreed that ye worship none but Him, and that
ye be kind to parents. Whether one or more attain old age in
thy life, say not to them a word of contempt, nor repel them,
but address them in terms of honour. And out of kindness,
lower to them the wing of humility, and say, 'My lord! Bestow
on them Thy Mercy, even as they cherished me in childhood.'
(Sura 17:23-24)

'I love the way this passage reminds us how important our parents
are. God commands us here to show kindness to our parents; it's
inspiring.' 'It reminds me of other Qur'anic passages where we are
instructed to honour our mothers,' Amina remarks. 'It's interesting
to think about it now when society seems to condemn women who
have chosen motherhood over a career.'

Usama is sitting to her left. Before she can finish he interrupts,
'I have to say, there are a couple of the Hadith[1] you have chosen
alongside this passage which I don't like. I think some of them justify
the neglect of children's rights.' At this point a Christian voice intervenes. Neil is from Sri Lanka; he heard about SR at university and has
come along with his friend Basim to check it out. 'Sorry, can you just
explain the difference between Sura and Hadith?' Amina explains and
the conversation returns to questions over some of Mounira's choices.
After a little while we move on to the Christian passage. Keith has
prepared some thoughts by way of introduction to Christian scriptures
about parenting. He reads from one of the epistles: 'Fathers, do not
exasperate your children; instead, bring them up in the training and
instruction of the Lord' (Ephesians 6:4). Keith talks about how 'flexible'
and open to interpretation the Bible is. He suggests that there are
different ways of interpreting some of the commandments regarding
parenting. I feel uncomfortable: I don't want the Muslims present to
think that we Christians are 'wishy-washy' liberals who shun difficult
passages in the Bible or simply interpret it in a way that suits us best.
But I've learnt that feeling uncomfortable is part of the point of SR as
it exposes the multiple readings of scripture, illuminating the different
interpretations within and between the texts of these religions.

The conversation continues around me as I reflect that in the past I probably thought that Christians should present a united front. SR has taught me that we speak as individual believers. Keith is not offering doctrinally conclusive Christian statements any more than Mounira is as a Muslim. He is talking about how the Word of God lives for *him,* revealed through the Christian scriptures. This is crucial. SR encourages us to enjoy the particularity of our different traditions, and even our own distinctive viewpoints within each of our traditions. Through this it builds an energy that directs us into one another's company.

Father Stephen, a curate in Bradford who was involved in establishing this group, put it succinctly when he was introducing the newcomers to the practice this evening. He told us, 'SR teaches us to disagree well. It builds a sense of friendship and hospitality. It models a way of living well in the city.' It isn't about presenting a neatly packaged religion, nor is it about collapsing our religions into a fourth, 'neutral' place. It's about finding the freedom to speak and study together from within our own tradition, and in so doing learning to disagree with others, Jewish, Christian or Muslim, and build friendships through that. There aren't many Jews in Bradford so for the time being this group has been Muslim–Christian. There is something quite remarkable about the way this Jewish practice is being received and developed by Muslims and Christians in Britain.

I rejoin the conversation as Pippa is using the texts to probe the topic of parenting a little further. 'It's interesting that the Qur'anic passages look at how children should treat their parents where the Biblical ones consider how parents should treat their children.' Usama nods in agreement: 'We have this growing problem in the Muslim community where parents are not thinking about what is best for their child, they are taking away the right of the child to choose – for example, who they marry. The way this passage emphasizes the rights of the child is helpful. British Muslims need to think about this.' At this moment our scriptural world is edging into our lived world as we consider what resources for living well together in Bradford might be found in our scriptures.

An interjection from Father Stephen brings the world directly into our study: 'One of the hardest things about my curacy has been knowing when it is appropriate to intervene and show kindness. I walk around the parish and see appalling things. I see parents abusing their children in public. And I don't know what I should be doing about it. How do I show kindness to those children when at a certain level it's none of my business?' I sympathize with Stephen. I'm tired of the way we feel we have to keep our mouths shut because we don't want to seem pushy or interfering. A soft Muslim voice interjects: 'Well, this is where faith comes in. What does faith teach us about helping people? I think our scriptures do call us to action. We need to work out how to be communities that care for one another once again.'

As our session concludes we find ourselves back with the Qur'anic emphasis on kindness. We bid our farewells, the group agrees to meet next month to look at the theme of justice and I find myself on the train back to Cambridge mulling over the insights gleaned from this evening's session. Through conversation with the Qur'anic scriptures and my co-readers, my scriptures have been opened up in new ways. Questions arise as I find myself led deeper into the Bible through my engagement with the Qur'an. In what ways am I as a Christian called to be kind? I hadn't appreciated the frustration some Muslims feel about attitudes towards arranged marriage. I haven't come away with any answers. Scriptural Reasoning never promises answers. I do, however, have the sense of having witnessed real friendship between people who, like me, believe that their scriptures have something important to say about the world in which we live.

SR from academy to world

The two SR sessions that I have described portray the different contexts in which the practice is developing. As outlined above, SR began amongst scholars in the university. Bradford is an example of a new context for SR as we began to ask whether the practice could be 'transported' beyond the academy. If it can, how do we use it constructively? Can SR really offer us a model for learning to live and work well together?

The experience of developing SR beyond the academy is sometimes described as the final stage of SR. As one member has observed, applying SR to the problems and issues that inspired SR practice in the first place is 'scriptural reasoning in action. It is scriptural reasoning as peace-making.'[2] There is an element of risk. We are aware that as we gather to read scripture we are people whose communities are often in conflict with each other. Through SR we seek to model the peace we hope and pray is to come. This can make us fearful, perhaps because it feels as though much is at stake.

People who have participated in sessions at conferences in America or in Cambridge find it hard to believe that SR could work in a non-academic, 'civic' context in the way that I experienced in Bradford. Doesn't one need scholars of New Testament Greek, of Tafsir or Midrash to practice SR? Our quest for 'SR in action' and for answers to these questions has proved explosive as well as peaceful. It is a practice that generates fear as well as friendship because learning to disagree well can be unsettling. In the civic context, without the apparent protection and control offered by the university, the fear factor seems to be more acute. The move from academy to civic space has highlighted critical features of SR if it is to thrive in the civic space, and it's important to tease out what is needed for the development of SR as a civic practice that might enrich our lives in communities of mixed religious and cultural traditions. The first involves the importance of community and the second is the need for leadership, for the role of a 'host'.

London

In 2004 a group began to meet at St Ethelburga's Centre for Peace and Reconciliation in the heart of the City of London to consider how SR might be developed to engage civic action. Academics from Cambridge and King's College London gathered with teachers, lawyers and clerics to develop SR as a community practice. These early experiences have been part of an ongoing experience that has helped clarify what makes 'SR in action' tick.

At St Ethelburga's our space was a tent, a beautiful goat's hair Bedouin tent designed in Saudi Arabia and erected at the back of the centre in 2006. Scriptural Reasoners have often used the tent as an image for the space they share when they gather to read scripture together. As a semi-permanent place the tent does not seek to replace our respective permanent religious houses. It symbolizes something of the fragility of such a gathering and it has scriptural resonances of hospitality and divine presence. The tent was thus in many ways the ideal space for friendships to flourish. Without becoming a permanent home for any of us, it provided the appropriate 'mutual' ground that SR seeks, neither neutral nor 'owned' by any one religion.

The early days of civic SR were exciting. People were inspired by what appeared to be a new way of engaging with members of different religious traditions, and friendships began to form. However, after a while some of the tensions and challenges created by SR came to the surface. Difficult power dynamics developed. Most of the problems seemed to be around organization and protocol rather than the practice itself. Without the academic 'cover' provided by the university context there seemed to be greater concern over doctrine and proper practice. We had no shared context other than the SR meeting itself. Questions of definition, of copyright, future development, and issues of propriety took over. We found ourselves embroiled in email battles about authority and ownership. Offence was easily taken. Friendships were broken and people got hurt. We became agonizingly aware of the fragility of SR. We found it so enriching; we longed to do it, yet we were fearful of the damage that it caused. The questions and arguments provoked by SR, which we had previously relished, became a source of threat and fear. Nothing had prepared us for when the differences overwhelmed us. It felt as though there was nothing and no one to contain the explosions. The imperative and indicative moods began to dominate our reading once again. Without the controlled community offered through the academy, people began to define doctrinal boundaries and reverted to making propositional statements. In the absence of the academic cover we realized there was a need for some kind of common context that could hold us in our differences.

SR beyond the academy: community and clerics

SR in community

To take the first of my two criteria for civic SR, 'community' is crucial, but it needn't be tied to location. It refers to the notion of other allegiances shared by the group that mean they are accountable to each other in other areas of their lives. The university provides one kind of community; Bradford offers another. I think that the sense of belonging to something else *together* meant that disagreements did not threaten the life of the group as they did at St Ethelburga's; rather, they enlivened it. Bonds had formed and people were learning to debate well together because the SR 'tent' was not the only thing uniting them. They belong to a community. They are neighbours. They meet on other occasions – at meetings of the Islamic Society of Britain, in church or at the school gate. They begin to see how their reading of scripture informs their lives together.

In contrast, at St Ethelburga's we drew people from all over London. We met for two hours once a month, returning afterwards to jobs and homes across the city. Making the vital connection between text and world was hard because we didn't share other worlds with our co-readers. This was particularly apparent when we faced problems. If things grew tough, people could just quit the group and we were unsure how to respond when an individual disrupted or dominated the session. When explosive elements threatened to erupt there was nothing beyond the flimsy fabric of the tent to contain them. The friendships were perhaps too fragile. Unlike Bradford or the academic groups, at St Ethelburga's we had little to do with each other beyond the monthly SR meeting. The temporary tent-like structure was the only thing holding us together and in a way we had set too much store by it.

The sense of belonging together to something else in addition to SR is important because the SR gathering should not seek to replace the religious traditions and other communities from which we come. At the end of the session the tent pegs are pulled up, the tent folded away and Reasoners return to their lives lived in communities. Where there is some other form of shared community, SR can provide a map for our other interactions. Learning to read together is only one part of the process; it helps us think about how we work and live together.

SR and clerics

If developing SR in community is really what the practice is about, I think it works best when facilitated by a host, and often the most appropriate person for the task is a religious leader. This is the second criterion for civic SR. But its development in the civic space relies on a relationship *between* academic and civic SR. It is in this transporting of SR to the heart of community that leadership from the cleric is valuable. Here we witness the role of the rabbi, imam or priest in making the transition from academic to civic SR. Experience has shown that an exchange between the university and the non-academic world can be extremely enriching for Scriptural Reasoning. The academic finds herself challenged by questions concerning text and world, and the civic group's study can be enriched by the scholarly expertise of the visitor.

The cleric can help facilitate this exercise of mutual learning. It was the experience of practising SR while he was training for ordination in Cambridge that inspired Father Stephen to introduce it in Bradford during his curacy. Drawing on theological training in scripture, doctrine and philosophy, the priest, rabbi or imam can bridge the gap between academy and world. He can face both ways: towards the scholarship of the traditions and towards the life of the community in which he ministers. Experience has taught us the need for leadership; it is a practice that needs champions. These groups don't begin organically and run themselves. The hosting offered by a cleric gives SR members the freedom to debate, discuss and disagree. Living at the heart of communities while remaining committed to scholarly engagement with the texts and traditions of the religion, the religious leader seems ideally suited to help guide the conversation.

To conclude, through both academic and civic SR I have developed some wonderful friendships, but they haven't been without their difficult moments. Reading with Muslims and Jews has taught me an enormous amount about my own faith. Our struggles together with our respective scriptures have given me a strong sense of the guiding presence of God. In different ways, my co-readers have changed the way I read the Bible. The mode of reading scripture encouraging question and debate is a gift from the Jewish tradition that has released me to enjoy the complexities and intricacies of the Bible rather than feel scared by them. The gift Islam has bequeathed is the way in which Muslims use scripture to instruct their lives. I am constantly inspired by my Muslim friends' knowledge of their Holy Book. The words of the Qur'an are literally on their lips and guiding their actions throughout the day. They have shown me something of what it means to believe that the Word of God is living and active discerning the thoughts and intentions of the heart.

There is something about SR that does help discern the way you think about the world. Before starting SR, I had never really sat down in conversation with a Jew. Growing up in the Arab world, I had plenty of Muslim friends and felt an affinity with Islam. However, despite sharing a large proportion of scripture with the Jewish tradition, I had a fairly one-sided, politically-driven antipathy towards the Jewish faith. Reading and learning from new Jewish friends has shown me the richness and holiness of a religion I have come to love and respect deeply. This has radically complicated my previously black-and-white feelings concerning the current crisis in the Middle East. SR does not provide us with answers; even better, it frees us to ask questions.

To bring the question back to Britain and our experiences here of inter-religious encounter, I now find myself thinking about what SR means for me today. God willing, I shall be ordained in a year or so and begin my three-year curacy in a parish in south London. I watch friends from seminary who have recently been ordained struggle with the 'interfaith issue'. The question of what to *do* with a group of Muslims, Christians, Hindus, Sikhs, Jews living side by side in their parish, but never giving one another the time of day, is one that challenges us all. We are tired of interfaith gatherings where people sit around drinking mint tea, eating samosas and agreeing that we are all the same really, or hearing for the hundredth time what the five pillars of Islam mean for Muslims. We are weary of the pressure to set and achieve outcomes, yet we know we have to do something. That is when I feel grateful for what I've learnt in Scriptural Reasoning. It is at heart a practice that brings people of faith together; we are doing something but we're not actually trying to *achieve* anything. We do it for God's sake, trusting that our respective scriptures have something to tell us about how we might learn, live and work together well.

In this sense, SR truly is a practice that belongs to the three traditions. Together we enrich our understanding of the Word of God and its place in our lives. SR celebrates the fearfulness and fragility of these complicated friendships and it encourages us to push through together, even when the odds of success seem to be stacked against it. As Keith from Bradford said to me, 'The thing is, it works. Things you think are complete barriers to understanding each other actually turn out not to be.'

Notes

1 The Hadith are the traditions and sayings of the Prophet Mohammed and his followers and form an important form of secondary text for the Muslim tradition.
2 David F. Ford and C. C. Pecknold (eds), *The Promise of Scriptural Reasoning* (Oxford: Blackwell, 2006), p. 25.

10

Hospitality in Prayer

Judith, SLG

Sister Judith tells the story of sharing silent prayer with her Muslim neighbours in East Oxford. She speaks of her inner resistances, of the depth of intensity of the shared prayer-experience, and of the discovery each of those praying makes: that this is about shared worship, and not about conversion. Each recognizes the holy in the other; together they encounter the same God.

As a nun who spends most of my time in the convent where I live, simply living and praying, privately in my cell and corporately and publicly in chapel, I don't have much direct contact with Muslims; even though the convent is set in the multi-faith context of East Oxford with the wonderful, cosmopolitan Cowley Road and its shops and restaurants from seemingly most Asian and European nations a stone's throw away. Yet as a nun, dedicated to opening my heart to the mercy of God and therefore in consequence to others, I have found a level of contact through prayer and a shared exposure to the mercy of God which has surprised me by its vitality and its similarity, though the paths be quite different.

In 2003 I was one of a group of sisters who visited a local mosque during Muslim Awareness week. It was newly built; the lower floor was complete, but the upper storey was still bare concrete. Our guide explained to us how this vast space and the dome above it would gradually be made beautiful and, in the course of doing so, he recited the Fatiha (the opening words of the Qur'an and of all formal acts of worship) in Arabic. I asked him for an English translation, and what struck me deeply, there and then, was the great similarity of its petitions with some of those contained in the Lord's Prayer. This encounter would later prove to be the first small step on a long journey of discovery.

Sickened by the events of 7 July 2005, I felt a need to join with the Muslims of the local area to do something positive. It was difficult – as a Christian, and a member of an enclosed monastic order – to think how this might be done. But in my favour was our charism of silent prayer, so I offered to organize an hour's silent prayer as part of 'One World Week'. Our local interfaith officer visited and gave me invaluable advice and some useful contacts. Thus I found myself getting in touch, out of the blue, with a whole host of people. The result was really heartening – about 30 visitors – and as one of the local Christians left he asked me, astounded to see two Muslims of different denominations, 'How did you get those two men to sit and pray together in the same room?' The answer was simple; I had invited them to share silent prayer together, having no idea that either would find the presence of the other a problem. But there they were, one Ahmadiya and one mainstream Muslim praying together, with Christians, at the invitation of a group of nuns in response to an act of violence which violated the heart of Islam.

In 2009 the Littlemore group decided on the title *Hospitality, Anglicanism and Islam* for its next conference. I felt that the only way I could engage with this title was at the level of prayer. So I decided to ask one of the imams who had come to the silent prayer for One World Week to teach me the Fatiha. I would use it and see where it took me. I also asked him to show me the actions that I associate with Muslims praying, and to explain their meaning, as I had a deep sense that I needed to use my body in prayer. The English translation of the prayer runs:

In the name of God, the most Beneficent, the Most Merciful
Praise belongs to God, the Sustaining Lord of all the Worlds
The Most Beneficent, the most Merciful

The Master of the Day of Judgement
It is You we worship, it is You we ask for help.
Show us the right way
The way of those whom You have blessed, who incur no anger
and are not astray.

Knowing that, for a Muslim, the prayer should be said in Arabic I
tried to learn it that way. So it was that I began my morning period
of prayer with '*Bismillah ir rahma nirrahim*' ('In the name of God, the
Most Beneficent, the Most Merciful'), and then bent to put my hands
on my knees and say '*Allahu akbar*' ('God is greater'), and then got
to my knees and touched first my nose and then my forehead on the
ground saying '*Subhan Allah*' ('Glory be to God').

This involved a great deal of inner opposition: 'Why are you
looking to another faith?'; 'Are you in danger of denying that everything necessary for salvation is found in Jesus Christ?'; and 'Are
you worshipping and bowing down to some strange god?' There
were unhelpful associations too: I have heard that those who flew
the planes into the Twin Towers did so chanting the words '*Allahu
akbar*'. This, in fact, provided me with a starting point. Perhaps,
by using the same words which they had used, I could begin to
create a bridge between two seemingly irreconcilable views of the
world, begin to reclaim those words to convey their truth, which felt
very much part of my community's vocation of reconciliation. The
Muslim and Christian worlds are frequently portrayed as being at
loggerheads, but what this 'hospitality' in prayer revealed to me was
much more common ground than many imagine there to be. In a
purely Christian way, I found it remarkably helpful to begin prayer
with the reminder that God is greater, especially as it was at this time
that I was told that a growth I had had removed had a one in three
chance of being a cancer.

The Fatiha goes on to speak of God being the Master of the Day of
Judgment, and that was in my mind as I said 'God is greater'. But God
is also my redeemer, and I was able to begin my prayers confident in
the assurance that God is greater than any of my failures in life or

prayer, simply remembering and giving thanks for my redemption. It was useful, too, to be reminded that God is greater than any concepts or imaginings I may come up with, however enlightening they may seem at the time.

A threefold declaration of 'Glory be to God' with my body was a real blessing, giving the whole of my body a chance to express itself prayerfully and with movement. William Dalrymple has suggested in his book *From the Holy Mountain*[1] that the early Muslims took their attitudes of body in prayer from the Christians around them, and that Eastern Christians have continued in that tradition. Could it be a blessing for Christians in the West to be reunited with their roots (and their Eastern counterparts) through contact with the Muslims around them?

At this time, it began to dawn on me that because Jesus calls God both 'Father' and 'the God of Abraham, Isaac and Jacob', the God we call 'Father' is also the 'God of Abraham, Isaac and Jacob'. The God of the Jews and the God of the Christians are one and the same. Jews and Christians may make different claims about Jesus, but they actually worship the same God. Wrestling with the inner accusation 'You are bowing down to some strange god' has brought to light for me the simple fact that 'Allah' is the Arabic word for God. It is not a name for God. The Qur'an describes God/Allah in ways that are extremely familiar to me: as the Creator and source of all being,[2] as being merciful, as being One,[3] as being the master of the Day of Judgement. So what came to me was that God is indeed One, as the Hebrew scriptures, the New Testament and the Qur'an assert. Islam may be another 'system' for expressing belief and life in God, but it is one and the same God that all three faiths talk about. I have often heard reference to the 'Abrahamic faiths', but would it be more helpful nowadays to assert that all three believe and worship one and the same God – to emphasize this, rather than Abraham, as our point of overlap?

Should I, as a Christian, break down my prejudices by theological examination of the nature and qualities of Allah as described in the Qur'an? Might I somehow be able to engage in this in a way that doesn't make me feel I am denying the uniqueness of the revelation we have been given in Jesus Christ? Receiving insights from another faith might be akin to the experience of reading the gospel in a language less familiar than my mother tongue, which can reveal new meanings or emphases.

I found that the exercise of 'hospitality' in prayer was enriching and challenging when it was done in the privacy of my cell. But I wondered it if could be done publicly. The imam spoke to me of a project he was involved in at a local school, providing mentorship for Muslim pupils and responding to the curiosity of non-Muslims regarding Islam. He conveyed very strongly the relentless sense of pressure he felt; how, walking down the street, he was aware of people passing him and wondering if he was a terrorist. This was hard for an adult to bear, he said, but how much more difficult it must be for the children. If somehow we could assert publicly that Christians and Muslims worship the same God, and if we could be willing to be hospitable enough in prayer to adopt practices not our own, might we begin to challenge the assumption that all Muslims are fanatics who wish us harm? And might we thus be living out something of Jesus' costly reconciliation?

I had been planning to organize some more silent prayer with the imam and Kaz, a local chip shop owner. He had been described to me as 'a most loving man', and indeed the chippy is rarely empty; all are welcome there, even if only to exchange pleasantries. He had come to see us on Good Friday, bringing an Easter card, and had run into me building the tomb for what was to be our Easter garden near the convent entrance. I thanked him for remembering our festivals, and he replied, 'Well, sister, it is like this. If you go into a man's house and mistreat his children he will get angry with you. And this [said with arms outstretched and looking up to the sky] is God's house and we are all his children.'

I wrote to the imam, Monowar, and explained that I would rather wait until I knew my pathology results and what treatment I might need, before I made a date for us to pray together. He replied as follows:

I am so sorry you have been unwell. Sadly, my cousin who was only 29 years of age, passed away on Tuesday; he'd been suffering from cancer of the spine. It has been a difficult week but at moments such as these, the Qur'an reminds Muslims to repeat the verse, 'Verily we are from God and to Him is our return.'

So do not worry about the meeting; we shall meet when God wills, as one of the Masters on the path has said, 'I discovered God through the failure of my plans.' In a world in which we are programmed to think that we are master of our destiny, it is only when we are confronted by the Will of God that we realize that true freedom comes only through adjusting our will/plan with the Great Plan.

So I pray for your good health and rapid recovery and look forward to meeting with you and Kazem.

In the meantime, take care, cherish each and every moment on your journey to God.

In peace,

Monowar

I fixed a date with Monowar, and went to the chippy to invite Kazem to join us in prayer. As usual, there were several people standing round chatting to Kaz. I issued my invitation and read him an extract from David Scott's poem 'Ibn Abbad Rose Early'. Written in the wake of 9/11, this seemed to articulate so well what we wanted to do:

All three went to Paradise,
Ibn Abbad, Rabbi Schmelke of Nikolsburg,
and Father Louis, and sat to eat
at the same table. They drank the water of life
and ate the meat of friendship. Whenever
their cups ran dry or their plates were empty
a little Nazarene came by and filled them up.

Who are you? they said.
I am Jesus, son of Mary. Can I sit awhile?
Be our guest, they said.

As they sat, the ground beneath them shook,
their faces paled and their eyes were filled
with knowledge, and with grief. *Today*
said Jesus *they will hate more and*
love more, than on any other day since the world began. Hold hands,
and ask our God to speak to us in Spirit. And there they sat
in love and prayer, all day,
Ibn Abbad, Rabbi Schmelke of Nikolsburg,
Father Louis, and Jesus, Mary's son.

and their silence was more profound than words
and their communion was most eloquent
and they willed the world to peace.

As I turned to leave, a man standing by the door said, 'You were speaking about praying with Kaz. Can I come too? I would like to visit the convent.' And so it was that Kamel joined our little group.

Kamel and Kazem arrived together. I explained to them that Monowar had taught me the Fatiha, and I hoped that we could start the silence with a recitation of it and end with the ringing of a little bell. Kaz replied, 'There are so many blessings in that prayer; it is an overflowing of the blessings of the merciful heart of God. There is a story which says that, if you look at it as an ocean, even all the angels couldn't carry the first wave of it because it is so big.'

He went on to explain, however, that it could be misunderstood. The last line, for example, speaks of those who are 'led astray'. This has sometimes been mistranslated as 'the lost', implying those who are beyond hope. But those who are led astray can be led back to the right path by example, by love. Even the devil was only misled – led astray by his jealousy on seeing God and wanting to be God. Even the

devil was beautiful and good, but misled into doing evil. I said that
this reminded me so much of St Isaac the Syrian:

> The human heart aflame for all creation, for humanity, birds,
> animals, demons and all creatures. As a person thinks of them
> their eyes overflow with tears. From the great and strong pity
> that grips their heart, and from the great suffering, their heart
> is wrung and it cannot endure, or listen to, or look upon any
> harm or the smallest sadness suffered by a creature. Therefore
> they pray incessantly in tears for the mute ones too, and for the
> enemies of truth, and for those who do them harm, that they
> may be kept safe and be forgiven; and also for the creeping
> things they pray with great pity, which is roused without
> measure in their heart, even likening them in this to God.

Kamel recited the Fatiha for us very beautifully, knowing the Qur'an
by heart. When he had finished I noticed that both he and Kaz made
a gesture with their hands rather like washing their face. I was worried
that this was something I should have done too. As the silence began I
sat on the floor, as is my custom for praying, and placed my copy of the
Fatiha beside me. The silence, for me, had all the usual depth of silence
in the presence of God. I noticed that Kaz in particular was reciting
prayers very quietly, but after a while he stopped. At the end of the
allotted time I rang the little bell. As I went to fetch us glasses of water, I
heard Kamel whisper to Kaz, 'It is so good to do something so different.'

As we were leaving, Kaz told me he had put my copy of the
Fatiha, which I had left by my cushion on the floor, on the highest
bookshelf and he pointed it out to me so that I would know where to
find it. He and Kamel came with me to compline, which they found
beautiful, and afterwards said that they wanted very much to come
back for some more silence next month. It wasn't until I retrieved
my copy of the Fatiha that I remembered that a Muslim would never
put the Qur'an, or any portion of it, on the floor, and I was touched
by Kaz's gentleness; he had not reproached me in any way, but had
simply guided me by example, just as he had said we should guide

others. When I thanked him for that at our next meeting, he smiled and said, 'The name of God always has the highest place.'

At our next meeting I asked Kaz about the gesture. He took my left hand and pointed to the lines ΛI on its palm and then showed me the IΛ on my right hand. He explained that the lines on my left had represented, in a certain script, the number 81, and the ones on my left 18. Added together they came to 99, and stood for the 99 beautiful names of God. The gesture they were making was with their palms upwards at the beginning, to receive these blessings, and then drawing them down, showering this light over them.

When Monawar arrived, he asked me if I had chosen this date knowing that today was a special day for them? I admitted that I had not, so he went on to explain that this was the day they kept the memory of Abraham's sacrifice of Ishmael. Somehow this led on to a discussion of Hagar's origins and the question of whether she was Egyptian. As there was a Bible in the room I offered to look it up, and found myself warmed that they were happy to accept what the Bible said. It seemed a bit ironic; a Christian and two Muslims consulting the Hebrew scriptures. Yet, as one of them pointed out, Abraham is the father of us all, so we are all cousins.

Again, the silence was beautiful and I found myself thinking, 'Where two or three are gathered together in my name, there I will be with them.' Yet we weren't exactly gathered in Jesus' name. I remembered that the question of conversion had come up at the Littlemore conference and realized that if either of these two had mentioned the thought of converting to Christianity I would have felt extremely uncomfortable. But surely I should want all to convert to Christ? It made me think that relationship to Jesus leads – or should lead – to growth in holiness. These men exuded holiness and it seemed to me, therefore, that God must already be working in them. What possible grounds could there be for conversion? Again they came to compline, and on the way they asked me about our time in chapel. They were interested to hear that sisters meet more than five times a day in chapel, and that our prayers vary according to the time of day.

A month later, whilst we were waiting for the group to assemble, there was some noise outside the room and Kaz asked me in a whisper what the other sisters thought about him and other Muslims coming here to pray. I told him honestly that some would find it difficult and others would be pleased.

Monawar arrived quite excited, with a bottle of Zam-Zam water which his father had brought back from a recent trip to Mecca. He explained that the water was special, from the well that Hagar's child had unearthed when she had left him desperate under a bush, and he invited us to share it. We all drank together, standing up according to tradition, and this sharing of sacred and precious water was more moving than I can say.

The silence was beautiful, and again they came to compline afterwards. They seemed to feel more at ease in chapel and asked me what was special about the chapel opposite where they were sitting (Our Lady chapel, where the blessed sacrament is reserved). I was warmed by their genuine interest and desire for reverence.

I was invited to attend Sunday service at a nearby parish where a local imam was going to address the congregation. His title was 'The close connectivity between Christianity and Islam'. He began by stressing that Islam is respectful of 'the people of the book' and tolerant of the two preceding faiths: 'Islam regards itself as an integral part of the Abrahamic family of faiths worshipping the very same sovereign God of the Torah and the gospels. So, whether you refer to the Lord of the universe by the biblical terms of Yahweh or Jehovah or by the Qur'anic name of Allah (which is the Arabic terminology for God), Muslims revere the *identical* Supreme Being that Jews and Christians venerate. In other words, Muslims believe in the *same* Lord of the heavens and the earth, the sole Creator of you and me and everything around us.' I was heartened by his expressing the same conclusion I was coming to and supporting it by quoting extensively from the Qur'an.

Next time only Kaz was able to come. While we talked, he told the story of how, before his death, Mohammad had prayed for the world, and how the cloak he was wearing had become soaked in his sweat. This was resonant of Jesus in Gethsemane and, as it was Passiontide,

I was particularly struck by this. Kaz spoke so passionately about his faith and said at one point, 'I don't want to convert you.' It hadn't occurred to me that he might want to, but I was glad that we could speak so frankly about this. Each of us was quite clear that our aim was to encourage the other's faith and practice of it.

After Easter, Monowar arrived bearing the gift of a book for the sisters on the Sufi science of self-realization. It is a practical book about living the spiritual life, which reveals much in common with the Christian Desert Father tradition. Having left it out for all sisters to see, I was greeted by two sisters in 48 hours who both said how much it had spoken to them.

I asked if there was a Muslim tradition of silent prayer. Monowar confirmed that this was so, particularly in the Sufi tradition. Kaz said that on the Day of Judgement God will only ask one question of each person: 'My servant, I have always been with you, you are always in my presence, who have you been with in your heart?' Just as in the Christian tradition, prayer is, at its most basic, being in the presence of God. God, who is limitless, nevertheless offers to make the human heart the throne of God. We all three sat in silence trying to allow that to happen. There was, prior to that, some heated and interesting debate about the wearing of the niqab, with Monowar and Kaz holding different opinions. When I said that I always tried to smile at a woman I passed who was wearing one, given that I too wear very similar garb, the response was 'Ah, the sisterhood of solidarity of the conspicuously dressed!'

Obviously this piece is a constantly evolving process, like stepping-stones across a river, and all I can do is describe each one as I tread on it. The monastic path calls us to enlarge our heart by simplicity of life and an attentiveness to listen to the voice of God through its prosaic detail. I hadn't expected when I began that this listening would bid me attend to another faith tradition, but I am finding my initial expectations were too narrow. I am enriched as my heart is stretched by attending to what one Muslim prayer can teach me of the mercy of God. As this unfolds, I become more aware that prayer requires me to lay aside my own fears, to draw nearer to my neighbour and be willing to open my heart to be enlarged; even to the extent of learning of God from another tradition. Then I can see that the God of whom another tradition speaks is the same God who calls me to faithfulness within my own.

Notes

1 William Dalrymple, *From the Holy Mountain* (London: Flamingo, 1998), p. 105

2 'He is the Originator of the heavens and the earth and when he decrees something, He says only "Be" and it is' (al Baqara 117).

3 'He is God the One, God the eternal' (al Ikhlaas 1-2).

Afterword

by the Archbishop of Canterbury

I

A question often asked when I meet with Sikhs and Hindus is what I think about 'conversion'. It's very clear that conversion is a sore point: members of these communities (to a lesser extent Buddhists too, and probably Jains and Zoroastrians) frequently feel that they are stuck in the middle of warring claims to universal truth represented by the two large Abrahamic bodies, Islam and Christianity, who are dedicated to prising them away from their allegiances and who are therefore challenging, at the most fundamental level, the legitimacy of what they say and do. They look on a good many interfaith initiatives with some scepticism: they are pretty sure that the superficial friendliness of Christians or Muslims conceals a basically hostile agenda. They are, many of them, convinced that their Abrahamic neighbours will never act disinterestedly and that these neighbours will use any means to cajole or bribe them away from their loyalties. The memory of 'rice Christians' dies hard in the folklore of South Asia. And they will speak with exasperation of their sense that they are sidelined in the public discussion of 'faith communities' and their place in society because they are habitually (in the UK) non-militant as well as non-proselytizing.

I begin with this point because I think it may help if we remember that the reciprocal fear between Muslims and Christians is only part of the picture: beyond that is the fear that is felt by other communities towards aggressive religious universalism. One of the saddest and most ironic results of the current global religious situation is the creation in India of a Hindu exclusivism expressed in violent aggression towards Islam and Christianity that simply mirrors the supposed aggression of its enemies, casting Hinduism as another determined religious system in a way that makes nonsense of most Hindu history. It seems we cannot think through either Muslim–Christian relations or the wider world of interfaith activity in this country without some rather longer thoughts about what religious universalism means.

Historically the point is clear enough. Christianity, it has been said, more or less invented the idea of 'religion' as something distinct from the sacral practices of this or that specific society; it took for granted that the community of believers had claims on the loyalty of its members that went far further than other claims of kinship or political identity. So when Manichaeism first appeared in Western Asia it was able to build on this idea of a universal truth and a community not limited by ethnic or local factors, and to construct itself as a network of relationships independent of these factors – in a way equally disturbing to both the great imperial powers of the region, Roman and Persian. And it was this background of universalism that in turn made possible the Islamic claim to a finality of revelation and a consequent universality of authority for the new revelation, expressed in the concept and the reality of an *umma*, a holy people, assembled around the revealed text, drawn from all races and classes, endowed with the common language of the holy text. Christians and Muslims alike represented (as did Manichees too in their day) a destabilizing presence in 'sacred' societies. They worked it out very differently – Islam through the close and intricate interweaving of religious law and political practice, Christianity through a complex and usually volatile attempt to balance parallel systems of power, 'church' and 'state'. But the underlying similarity should not be obscured: both claimed (and claim) that they are in some sense the optimal form of human sociality itself, a claim that is significantly different from what other religious traditions assume. And because of this, they are innately 'proselytizing' bodies, it seems.

Which at first sight suggests not only that Hindus and others are right to be worried, but that the relation between Islam and Christianity is inevitably a zero-sum game.

The essays in this book make it clear that in practice this is not what it feels like; but it would be a very rare participant in interfaith discussion who did not at some point feel the pressure of this question of universality. At some level, we can't *not* register that the reason we're talking to each other at all is that we have convictions about how things actually are; and if we have convictions about this, we naturally assume that all human beings will somehow have to come to terms with the same reality sooner or later. In a way, even the Hindu has that conviction – a sometimes passionate belief that the truth of the universe is irreducibly plural at the level of appearance and inexpressibly one in its depths, and that the two orders cannot be confused or assimilated. It won't do to say, 'I think it's like this, you think it's like that; who knows? And ultimately we may both be equally right or equally wrong.' That isn't the sort of attitude that changes anything much; and Islam and Christianity have certainly set themselves to change things in social habits and mores.

And just to complicate this even further, remember that what may sound like theoretical claims to universal truth are normally heard in the context of very non-theoretical power relations. As I've argued elsewhere, the question of 'religious offence' may sound like a plain issue of freedom of speech; but in fact it is regularly bound up with issues of power. The freedom to offend is rather different when exercised by a subaltern voice against a dominant one, from when a powerful majority exercises its liberty to offend a minority who feel they have no redress. A lack of trust – and, indeed, friendship – between majority and minority means that this latter kind of freedom of utterance is experienced as a plain intensification of injustice. And yet the sense of being 'blackmailed' into silence by what is seen as a hyper-sensitive minority adds another twist to the pattern – the characteristic resentment of the powerful towards the powerless when the powerless use whatever tools they have to hand. Too few discussions of blasphemy and offence seem to explore these dynamics. But they are part of the same set of questions around universalism. The anger and hurt of Muslims faced with what they see as offence is rooted in the perception that a secular public discourse is claiming a normative and unchallengeable status, a universal authority which entitles its speakers to declare open season on the convictions of a religious minority. To move this on towards a positive valuation of vulnerability (as Christians rightly want to) is quite a task if the presenting feeling is one of a pervasive frustration at being the target of unthinking mockery. We have after all been here in the history of how other groups have had to negotiate public mockery – women, gay people, particular ethnic communities. There is something about any uneven relation of power that ought to make us think rather hard about what freedom of speech means, not as an abstract value (which few would contest) but as a quite specific tool of communication, a quite specific way of expressing the actual social relations that prevail.

Hindus, Sikhs and others are afraid of 'Abrahamic' universalism. Christians and Muslims are afraid of each other's universalism. Everyone is afraid of secular universalism. That's rather a lot of fear, and we ought to be starting by now to think of how we can move beyond this, not only into friendship but into some sort of positive discourse of human solidarity. Because that is after all the immensely creative aspect of universalism – the belief that human beings ultimately have the same dignities, the same possibilities, that the good of any one part of the human family is bound up with that of all others. A world without universalisms of various sorts would have a lot more difficulty in tackling those problems that are not only, here and now, too complex for any one faith community or any one nation state to manage but also matters that affect those still unborn, with whom, on a religious basis, we have the same solidarity in principle. And I think that the question then becomes how we move the language of universal claim away from that of universal power, in such a way that an unqualified solidarity can be affirmed without it appearing as a bid for total hegemony.

When I am asked the sort of question I referred to at the beginning of these remarks, what I most want to say is this. Any 'conversion' that is the result of manipulation, force, threat or whatever is bound to be unreal. The only conversion that matters is a recognition that *here*, in *these* relationships to God and humanity, I am able to be who I am created to be. Or perhaps, more accurately, I discover something already true about myself, a solidarity I had never sensed before. Something is given before I take any step. When Jesus heals the ten lepers in Luke 17, one returns, recognizing what his healing entails for him. The rest are healed but do not at this point come to that recognition. Conversion is a recognizing that this is the appropriate response to what is already unconditionally bestowed. And in Christian terms, one focal aspect of what is already bestowed is the self-identification of God with every person through the assumption of human nature by the divine Logos. Christ's incarnation creates a universal solidarity; and its healing effect is at work whether or not it is recognized and celebrated. The Church is, absurdly, both necessary and unnecessary. It cannot help being there because the response of the tenth leper is an uncontrollable outpouring of thanks and a desire to be where thanks is given to God in Christ. And at the same time, the Church is 'unnecessary' in the sense that it is not the cause of God's healing action, God's solidarity. It simply announces that God is already healing all and in solidarity with all, and that here is a space in which that solidarity can be embraced and imagined and woven into the texture of a healed and healing life. Conversion is not the cause of healing but the response to it. If healing is not embraced in this way, it does not stop (the nine lepers do not have their leprosy back as a punishment), but we do not know how it works itself out in the transformation of particular lives. We have to be agnostic about how exactly this might work; and it is important not to talk about this as if healing were impersonal, automatic, unconnected in its outworking with the specific graces given in the community of belief, the community that is both necessary and unnecessary.

I think that a lot of the reflection in these essays is about a community that is both necessary and unnecessary in this way. The authors are trying to find ways of saying that the Church is not, even when manifestly weak and in a minority position, a dispensable presence. The bare fact of its existence declares a universal solidarity that allows it to engage in just those probing but not aggressive explorations into the sensitivities of its neighbours described so effectively in these pages again and again. The Church assumes (and it is no small assumption) that it has the authority to ask questions of all – even to ask questions of the powerless and offended that just might be transformative. The only thing that can make this less than arrogant is a language and practice that is dedicatedly *not* seeking control, that is seriously exploring friendship as a category of relations between equal partners in conversation, and thus attempting to give power and security to its partners. Thus a practice that arises from a conviction of given, universal solidarity offers a universalism that is gift not threat: the assurance of a place.

There is no way of avoiding the fact that conversion happens; and that the Christian, recognizing that some sort of conscious relationship with Christ is fundamental for the reality and continuance of the practice we have been sketching, can hardly discourage, let alone rule out, such a movement. But the Church somehow has to find a way (echoing Bonhoeffer's famous remark about how the language of Jesus changes things and our ecclesial speech generally doesn't) of acting so that it invites recognition of the gift without manipulating that recognition; of being manifestly a place where human healing is realized and celebrated but without sticking a price tag onto this. The price that matters, after all, has been paid long since.

As I suggested, this is to make quite a large claim. If we do indeed want to make our encounters with other faiths – not only Islam – something other than a zero-sum game, but do not want to settle down with a lazy relativism, we are in fact going to be saying that we cannot see ourselves as competing, one faith alongside others, one way among others to a distant and mysterious God. We do continue to make the ambitious claim that the universe is oriented to and around the Word who was flesh in Jesus. What that means, though, is that it is not for us to consume our energy in the anxiety to *create* the healing or solidarity we speak of in such a way that obliges the non-Christian to submit to the demonstration of power. As Paul says in *I Corinthians*, the power is not in our performance. And perhaps that begins to address the fear Christians can so readily be persuaded to feel: have I done enough, have I been clear enough about the uniqueness of Christ, have I 'offered Christ' effectively? They are serious enough questions, in all conscience, and in one way or another they need asking. But we also need to be delivered from the fear that God is impotent without our words.

The Church of England appears in these pages once again as having the advantages and disadvantages of a 'weak establishment'. It is simply and statutorily *there*, irrespective of the local popular vote. What these essays implicitly ask is how it can sustain the claim to universal pertinence in such a setting without plunging into straightforward competition. And the narratives set out here begin to answer that question, often movingly. If our situation in the Church of England does enable the beginnings of such an answer, my contention in this brief response to the more substantive pieces gathered here is that – not for the first time – our Church may find that it has articulated something that is significant for the Church as such, something about what the universality of Christ's claim does and doesn't look like in a practice that refuses the fantasy of universal control. Whether that makes dialogue continue more fruitfully or simply confirms the suspicion in some quarters that (Anglican) Christianity in the UK is just not robust enough remains to be seen. But I don't think I am the only contributor to this book to believe with intense conviction that sustaining a universal claim about healing and meaning without resorting to the tools of control or manipulation is a robust enough calling that takes a lifetime to learn.

A Note on the 2009 Littlemore Conference at St Andrew's, Handsworth

Edmund Newey

The Littlemore Group met for its third biennial conferences in the parish of St Andrew, Handsworth, in Birmingham, from 17 to 20 August 2009. It was a happy coincidence that the parish was celebrating the centenary of the completion of its beautiful, Grade I listed church building, and the conference formed part of a year-long series of events, ranging from the creation of a community artwork to a sponsored walk from the parish to the source of our water supply in mid-Wales.

The conference was widely experienced as a blessing. To group members it was a welcome return to the parochial context of our first gathering in 2005, reminding us of the rewards, challenges and needs found in the more diverse and deprived corners of the nation. To the guest speakers, Muslim and Christian alike, it gave the opportunity to share and receive insights in an environment that was companionable and unthreatening. To the host parish, it was an affirmation that Handsworth matters, that places like this have unique things to bring to the life of the body of Christ.

Our deliberations took place in the firm grasp of worship and devotion: the Eucharist, the daily office and silent prayer. Just as importantly, they incorporated time for companionship over food and drink, for refreshment in the open air and for inspiration through music and poetry. We were grateful to the Kopper Khazana restaurant in Handsworth and to Viva Baguettes for their care in catering; to the musicians from Lichfield Cathedral, Robert Crinson and Clare Graves; to Denise Inge for giving us 'An Evening with Thomas Traherne'; to the Sisters of the Love of God and the Divinity Faculty of the University of Cambridge for their generous sponsorship; and to numerous members of the congregation at St Andrew's for the kindness and help.

Those who took part in the conference were Liaqat Ali, Javaad Alipoor, Stephen Cherry, Sarah Coakley, Sarah Gill, Alex Hughes, Denise Inge, John Inge, Sr Judith SLG, Catriona Laing, Philip Lewis, Rachel Mann, Imran Manzoor, Jessica Martin, Miriam Mushayi, Edmund Newey, Abdullah Sahin, Andrew Shanks, Richard Sudworth, Ian Wallis, Frances Ward and Pete Wilcox.